The Art
of
the Celts

The Art of the Celts

ORIGINS  HISTORY  CULTURE

Iain Zaczek

PB

PARKGATE
BOOKS

Acknowledgments

many people have assisted me in the writing of this book. Ian Chilvers and Valerie Levitt offered generous help in finding elusive, out-of-print books and in solving an assortment of knotty problems. In their different ways, the following have also provided me with advice, encouragement or inspiration – Françoise Sciré, Valmai Adams, Gillian Chaplin, James Collenette, Diane Dewar, Caroline Juler, Stephen Marsh, Helen Mowat, Diane Page, Sarah and Emerson Peart, and Peter Simpson. Particular thanks must also go to Michael Jacobs, who inadvertently started me off on the Celtic trail.

First Published in Great Britain in 1997
by Parkgate Books Ltd, London House,
Great Eastern Wharf, Parkgate Road,
London SW11 4NQ

Text copyright © Parkgate Books Ltd

British Library Cataloguing in Publication Data:
A CIP catalogue record for this book is available from the British Library.
ISBN 1–85585–322–1

1 3 5 7 9 8 6 4 2

Edited, designed and typeset by
Book Creation Services Ltd, London

Printed and bound in Hong Kong by Dah Hua

❖ Contents ❖

Background

F ew civilizations have exerted a more lasting influence than that of the Celts. Their culture flourished in Europe before the Romans built their Empire and before Christianity took root, and, yet, it remains a living force to this day. Celtic languages are still spoken in Brittany, in Ireland, and in parts of the British Isles, and the visual appeal of early Celtic design remains as potent as ever.

The sheer scope of the Celtic world may surprise some people, for it endured for over a millennium – from around the 6th century B.C. to the 9th century A.D. During this lengthy period, the fortunes of the Celts ebbed and flowed, and although they always remained a group of loosely knit tribes and never formed a coherent nation, their power extended over most parts of Europe at one time or another. At their peak, they were mighty

Statue of a warrior, from Vachères, France, 1st century A.D.

Wooden bucket with bronze mounts from Aylesford, England, 1st century B.C.

enough to overrun the strongholds of Rome (386 B.C.) and Delphi (279 B.C.). Even when their military strength waned, the impact of their culture lingered on, imprinting itself on the style of early Christian artworks.

The precise origins of the Celts are shrouded in mystery. The earliest mention of the word *keltoi*, used by Greek writers to describe a people living in the Upper Danube region, occurred in the 6th century B.C. Despite this, it is clear that certain facets of Celtic civilization date back much further. Many authorities have seen rudimentary traces of it in the late Hallstatt era or, more exactly, in the Hallstatt D period (c.600 B.C.–c.450 B.C.). Its full development, however, took place in the following era, the La Tène period, which lasted from c.450 B.C. to c.50 B.C.

Both Hallstatt and La Tène refer to important prehistoric sites, which have yielded vital archaeological evidence. Hallstatt is situated in Austria, some 225 km southwest of Vienna. In ancient times, this remote spot was a thriving commercial centre, the result of the salt mines in the area. Revealing clues about the community that worked here have been unearthed from Hallstatt's cemetery, which was discovered by Johann Georg Ramsauer in 1846. Ramsauer was a mining surveyor and, over the course of the next 17 years, he undertook detailed excavations, uncovering almost a thousand graves. He carefully noted down all the artefacts that came to light and arranged for watercolours to be made at each site, recording the exact position of every find.

From a Celtic perspective, the most intriguing discoveries were made in Grave 994. Here, a warrior was interred along with his weapons, helmet and a wine sieve. Much attention has been focused on the man's bronze scabbard, which includes engraved depictions of horsemen and foot-soldiers. Their weapons and armour relate closely to finds in other Celtic graves, and the stylized portrayal of the horses – most notably, the 'teardrop' shape of their haunches – provides a telling foretaste of the La Tène style.

Comparable finds have been made at a series of princely graves in central and western Europe, mostly dating from the 6th century B.C. At Hirschlanden in southern Germany, archaeologists recovered a remarkable funerary statue, a torc-wearing warrior carved out of sandstone. In eastern France, there were equally spectacular finds at the fortified settlement of

Mont Lassois, culminating in the discovery of the tomb of the princess of Vix (c.500 B.C.), which was excavated in 1953. Chief among her belongings was a massive torc, made of solid gold, and an impressive array of bronze drinking vessels.

Detail of bronze mount from the Aylesford bucket, England, 1st century B.C.

The most impressive site of all, however, is the tumulus at Eberdingen-Hochdorf, not far from Stuttgart. Here, a prince was interred on a unique burial couch, formed out of six plates of gilded bronze. The backrest was decorated with military scenes, while the couch itself was supported on eight castors shaped like dancing girls. A series of feasting vessels were placed nearby, among them a set of nine drinking horns and a large bronze cauldron, adorned with figures of lions.

A high proportion of the articles in these tombs were either imported or were made locally by foreign craftsmen. Even so, they indicate the early presence in the Celtic heartlands of the many and varied artistic strands, which would eventually come together to form the distinctive style that we now associate with the Celts. In particular, they confirm a fondness for Greek and Etruscan wares, coupled with tantalizing hints of Eastern influences. The latter can be deduced from fragments of silk clothing, found on some of the deceased, and from artefacts like the Syrian mirror, which was discovered in a tomb at Grafenbühl.

The true blossoming of Celtic art occurred during the La Tène era. Like Hallstatt, this takes its name from a remarkable archaeological site, which has revealed finds that are typical of the age. La Tène is located in Switzerland, not far from the northernmost point of Lake Neuchâtel. Here, in 1857, the first discoveries were made by an antiquary called Hansli

Kopp. He found a cache of around 40 iron weapons deposited in the water, close to a series of submerged wooden piles.

The site received further attention after 1868, when work began on a scheme to regulate the level of water in the Jura. At this stage, La Tène was drained completely and thorough excavations were carried out. In due course, this led to the discovery of some 270 spears, 170 swords, a variety of jewellery, and a scattering of human and animal bones. The preponderance of weapons gave rise to the theory that La Tène had once been a prehistoric arsenal, but the precise nature of the site has never been fully ascertained. Recent observers tend to the view that it was a sacred place, where precious objects were thrown into the water as votive offerings. If so, then the bones may be the residue of more sinister sacrifices. Whatever the truth, the scale and quality of the finds have caused the name of La Tène to be adopted as a type site, representing the high watermark of Celtic achievement.

Since the La Tène era covers such a huge span of time, the period is usually subdivided into a number of different stylistic phases. Several different systems have been mooted, ranging from a simple 'Early', 'Middle', and 'Late', to a more descriptive 'Strict Style', 'Free Style', 'Free Graphic', and 'Free Plastic Style'. However, the notation that is still most commonly used is the one devised back in the 1940s by Paul Jacobsthal. He identified four distinct tendencies in Celtic art: 'Early Style', 'Waldalgesheim Style', 'Plastic Style', and 'Hungarian Sword Style'. These very broad

Sword from a Hallstatt grave, 7th century B.C.

categories are helpful, even though they cannot be regarded as a reliable guide to dating. This is partly because the periods overlap considerably, and partly because individual styles reached different parts of the Celtic world at different times.

The Early Style emerged after c.480 B.C. and is typified by the finds made in a series of rich, princely graves in France and Germany. The most notable sites include Reinheim, Rodenbach, Basse-Yutz, and Kleinaspergle. Essentially, the style is a fusion of three separate elements: classical, oriental, and Hallstatt. The classical motifs came from Greece and Etruria, and consisted mainly of such forms as tendrils, lyres, lotus buds, and palmettes. Unlike their classical counterparts, however, the Celtic versions of these motifs were rendered in a loose and flowing manner, a foretaste of the swirling patterns that were to develop later.

From Hallstatt, the early Celtic craftsmen derived a repertoire of geometrical designs, along with some of their animal imagery. The oriental contribution is much more elusive. Here, the principal sources appear to have been Scythian or Persian. The latter was particularly influential, following the campaigns of King Darius in the 6th century B.C., which brought the Persian armies as far as Thrace. This Eastern connection is most apparent in the Celtic taste for exotic animals, such as griffins, ibexes and S-shaped dragons.

The next phase is known as the Waldalgesheim Style (emerging after c.350 B.C.), which coincides with the period of the great Celtic expansion. This brought Celtic settlers into Greece and Italy. Waldalgesheim takes its name from an outstanding burial site in Germany. Here, a princess was interred with her consort, amid a fine array of chariot fittings, jewellery, and elaborately decorated household wares. Jacobsthal regarded this as the classic period of Celtic design and also described it as the Mature Style. Nowadays, however, it is more commonly known as the Vegetal Style. As this suggests, plant imagery played a dominant role in the designs, usually taking the form of winding tendrils or wreaths. Often, stylized human faces would also be present, half-concealed amid the foliage. Coral, too, began to feature more prominently in decorations and red enamel came into use for the first time.

Pedestal vase from Prunay, France, late 4th/early 3rd century B.C.

Bronze wine flagon from Basse-Yutz, France, 4th century B.C.

The influence of the Waldalgesheim Style spread far beyond Germany, and some of the finest examples have been found in Celtic graves in northern Italy.

After this came the Plastic Style, which flourished from around 290 B.C. Two new features were introduced during this period: firstly, craftsmen began to model their artworks in much greater relief, moving away from the two-dimensional forms that had been popular in the previous era. These bulkier shapes were also notable for their extravagant, asymmetrical designs. In addition, artists displayed a growing interest in human and animal forms. Often, these were treated playfully, with a blend of humour and fantasy, but they could also be disquieting, combining grim expressions with fierce, bulging eyes. Most of these attributes can be found in the fine collection of bronze mounts which came to light in 1941 at Brno-Malomërice, during construction work on the local railway station.

Detail of monster from Basse-Yutz flagon.

The final tendency identified by Jacobsthal was the Hungarian Sword Style, now known simply as the Sword Style. This was in evidence from the end of the 2nd century B.C. and, as might be expected, it is characterized by the weaponry of the period. After the brilliant, three-dimensional forms of the previous age, Celtic craftsmen now returned to a flat, linear style, reserving their finest designs for the decoration of iron swords and scabbards. The format of these patterns appears to have stemmed directly from the Waldalgesheim manner. Despite the initial link with Hungary, the greatest concentration of finds has occurred in Switzerland, many of them at La Tène itself.

As the La Tène era drew to a close, Celtic tribesmen still controlled large tracts of continental Europe, but this was soon to change. In 58 B.C., Julius Caesar embarked on his campaigns in Gaul, which culminated in the defeat of Vercingetorix at Alesia in 52 B.C. Then, under Augustus, the region was divided into four provinces and was rapidly assimilated into the Roman Empire. Some practices, such as druidism and human sacrifice, were outlawed completely, while others were incorporated smoothly into the Roman system of belief. This much is evident from the celebrated altar of Reims (1st century A.D.), which depicts the Celtic god, Cernunnos, sitting between Apollo and Mercury.

A similar state of affairs existed in the East. Octavian sent an invading force into Pannonia (which included parts of present-day Hungary, Austria and Slovenia) in 35 B.C., and Roman power in the region was consolidated by the annexation of Noricum (Austria) in 15 B.C. Once again, local citizens were encouraged to adopt the customs and beliefs of their new masters. Inevitably, the process of Romanization engulfed many of the old La Tène traditions, although they did survive, in varying degrees, in the outlying areas of the Empire.

This influence was strongest on the western fringes of the continent, in the seven Celtic 'nations', which consisted of the remoter parts of Britain (Wales, Scotland, Cornwall, the Isle of Man), Ireland, Brittany, and Galicia in northern Spain. Although they had never wielded the same power as their ancestors from the La Tène era, the Celts in these last outposts did manage to preserve the essence of their ancient traditions. In Ireland, in particular, many aspects of Celtic culture survived long into the Christian era, largely because the island had always remained outside Roman control.

The spread of Christianity brought fresh opportunities for Celtic artists. Britain and Ireland were converted to the new faith in the 5th and 6th centuries, through the efforts of such pioneers as St Columba, St Patrick and St Ninian. They helped establish a Church that enjoyed an unusual degree of independence from Rome; one that was centred around a group of quasi-autonomous monastic communities. The most notable of these – places such as Iona, Durrow, Lindisfarne, and Kells – set up their own workshops, producing illuminated manuscripts and other items of liturgical equipment. Many of these featured the swirling, curvilinear designs that had been used by craftsmen throughout the La Tène era.

The comparative independence of the Celtic Church did not last for long. At the Synod of Whitby in 664, the full authority of Rome was recognized and its administrative practices were adopted. By a strange twist of fate, this only served to prolong the life of Celtic traditions. For the monastic artists of Britain and Ireland were now given the task of producing more religious artefacts, to aid in the conversion of northern Europe. The need for Biblical texts was particularly pressing and many books were sent out from Rome, to be copied in British and Irish monasteries. These manuscripts were then taken by missionaries to the Continent, where their influence spread rapidly. The books themselves are generally described as 'Insular', since it is often hard to gauge precisely where in the British Isles they were made.

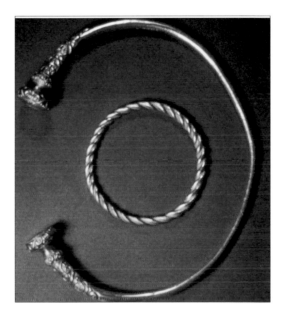

Gold bracelet and torc from Waldalgesheim, Germany, 4th century B.C.

The treasures made for the Christian Church provided a glorious coda to the Celtic era, which survived longest in Ireland, until it was eventually extinguished by marauding Vikings in the 8th and 9th centuries. Even after this, various aspects of Celtic culture were revived at periodic intervals. In the Middle Ages, for example, the Arthurian cycle of legends derived many of its most colourful details from Celtic source material. Then, during the Renaissance, the rediscovery of classical texts awakened fresh interest in the early history of the Celts, even if much of the attention was directed towards the ghoulish practices of head-hunting and human sacrifice. The 18th century witnessed the discovery of a number of important archaeological finds, but their significance was largely overshadowed by the publication of James Macpherson's *Ossian*. This spurious collection of 'ancient' Celtic texts was later discovered to be a fraud but, even so, it created a nostalgic craze for a mysterious, windswept past. 'Celtomania' spread across Europe, becoming one of the principal ingredients of the Romantic movement.

Arm-ring from the grave of the Waldalgesheim princess, 4th century B.C.

All subsequent attitudes to the Celts have been coloured to some extent by this Romantic image, making it harder for historians to unravel the secrets of their culture. Their task has been further complicated by the fact that the Celts left virtually no written records about themselves. The practice of writing was discouraged by the druids. As a result, Celtic scholars have been obliged to rely heavily on the accounts left by classical authors. These texts offer fascinating insights into some aspects of Celtic life, but they can also be biased and misleading. In general, the picture that emerges is of a proud and warlike people, who loved feasting, boasting and eloquence. They were fond of display and had – in the eyes of their adversaries, at least – a positive obsession with gold and fine jewellery.

Inevitably, the first priority of most classical commentators was to analyse the Celts' abilities as warriors. Diodorus Siculus, writing in the 1st century B.C., described how they liked to taunt their opponents before entering into combat: 'When the armies are drawn up in battle-lines, they will often advance and challenge the bravest of their opponents to single combat, brandishing their weapons all the while, so as to terrify their foe.

And, when someone accepts their challenge, they loudly recite the deeds of valour performed by their ancestors while, at the same time, abusing and belittling their opponent, attempting to rob him of his fighting spirit.'

In his *Commentaries* on the Gallic War, Julius Caesar confirmed this psychological approach, noting how the chief warriors used to utter terrible shrieks, while careering around in their chariots, in the hope of unnerving their foes. 'First, they drive about in all directions hurling spears. Generally, their opponents are thrown into confusion by the fearful noise of the horses' hooves and the rattle of the wheels. Then they leap down from their chariots, to fight on foot. Their charioteers, meanwhile, draw a little way off and position themselves, so that they can return for their masters, if the fighting should go against them ... In this way, they combine the mobility of cavalry with the staying power of infantry.'

Classical authors also explained how some classes of warrior used to go naked into battle, believing that this would offer them some form of supernatural protection, but the subject that preoccupied them most was head-hunting. A passage in Strabo's *Geography*, for example, reported: 'There is that custom, barbarous and exotic, that is common to many of the northern tribes ... that when they depart from battle they hang the heads of their enemies from the necks of their horses and, having brought them home, nail the spectacle to the entrance of their houses.'

Diodorus Siculus elaborated on this theme: 'The heads of their most illustrious enemies, they embalm in cedar oil and preserve in a chest. These they show off to strangers, solemnly maintaining that either they or one of their ancestors had refused to part with it, even when offered a large sum of money in exchange. Some of them, we are told, boast that they have refused its weight in gold, thereby displaying a barbarous sort of greatness; for not to sell the proofs of one's valour is a noble thing.'

There is little doubt that such tales were substantially true. When the Roman general Postumius was slain by Boii tribesmen in 216 B.C., they cut off his head, cleaned it out and gilded the skull. Then they used it as a vessel in their rites, believing that it was a source of great power. Archaeologists have found evidence of similar ritual activity at Entremont and Roquepertuse, two Gaulish shrines in southern France. Here, they discovered gruesome head-pillars with niches, where carvings of severed heads or genuine skulls were placed and revered. The fact that fragments of a war javelin were still embedded in one of these skulls makes it clear that the heads belonged to slain warriors, rather than sacrificial victims.

The broader religious beliefs of the ancient Celts are much less easy to determine. Surviving images suggest that they must have had a sizeable pantheon of gods, but a mere handful of names are known to us. Even Cernunnos, one of their most widely worshipped deities, can only be firmly linked with a single inscription. Here, classical sources are of little use. Caesar made a list of the principal gods, but he neglected to give the native names, using their Roman equivalents instead. 'The god they worship most is Mercury ... They see him as the inventor of all the arts, the guide of all their roads and journeys, and the god who has greatest power for commerce and money-making. After Mercury, they worship Apollo, Mars, Jupiter, and Minerva ...'

Mercury, in this instance, can probably be identified with Lugh. His role as a craft god equates well with 'the inventor of all the arts', and the considerable number of places that owe their name to him confirms the wide extent of his worship. Among others, they include Lyons (or Lugudunum) and Laon in France, Leiden in Holland, Liegnitz in Silesia, and Carlisle (or Luguvallum) in England. In Irish legend, he was also referred to as Lugh-chromain ('little stooping Lugh'), which later became anglicized as 'leprechaun'. The broad range of Lugh's influence underlines the fact that the Celts, while always lacking political unity, were still bound together by common cultural ties.

Some of these bonds were cemented by the Celtic holy men. Caesar divided the latter into three distinct classes – the vates (soothsayers), the bards and the druids. Of these, the druids were unquestionably the most important. Their duties included the supervision of various rituals, such as

Celtic craft god, found in East Anglia.

sacrifices and the interpretation of auguries, but their overall role extended far beyond this. They were also judges, teachers, advisers and astronomers. Kings and chieftains bowed to their authority, and their preachings about the transmigration of the soul inspired Celtic warriors to great feats of bravery, since they had no fear of dying in battle.

Modern notions about the druids have been much distorted, partly because of the undue emphasis placed on their sacrificial practices by classical writers, and partly because of their reinvention by French and English nationalist groups in the 18th century. In truth, very little is known about them. Their insistence on transmitting all knowledge orally meant that much of their culture died with them, when they were suppressed by the Romans. The few fragments that have survived suggest that their learning may have been considerable. The most impressive of these remains is the Coligny Calendar (2nd c. B.C.), which was discovered in 1897. Engraved on a large bronze tablet, this Gaulish calendar lists 62 consecutive months, covering a five-year period. These were calculated on both a lunar and solar basis, reconciling the waxing and waning of the moon on one hand with the length of the solar year. Individual sections of the months were described as 'mat' (good) or 'anm' (not good), which may mean that the calendar was used for divinatory purposes, indicating the most auspicious times for undertaking certain actions. In any event, the complexity of the calendar gives the lie to those ancient authors, who dismissed the Celts as brave but ignorant barbarians.

In artistic terms, the Celts displayed a similar degree of sophistication in their metalwork. From an early stage, the smith enjoyed a privileged position in society and was accorded special burial rites. Indeed, his ability to create a dazzling variety of objects and designs out of simple metal ores seemed almost magical to his contemporaries. Figurines of smith-gods have been unearthed at a number of sites – the most complete example originating from Sunderland in northern Britain – and images of anvils, tongs and hammers have been found on fragments of pottery. In addition, because his materials had to be extracted from the ground, his worship was frequently associated with the underworld. In Ireland, for example, the chief smith-god was Goibhniu, whose secondary role was to preside over banquets in the Otherworld. The supreme skills of the smiths and metalworkers were already apparent in the Hallstatt swords, which were produced at the dawn of the Celtic era, and can still be detected on their final masterpieces, the lavish shrines and chalices of Christian Ireland.

Gaulish coinage, Bellovaci staters,
3rd/2nd century B.C.

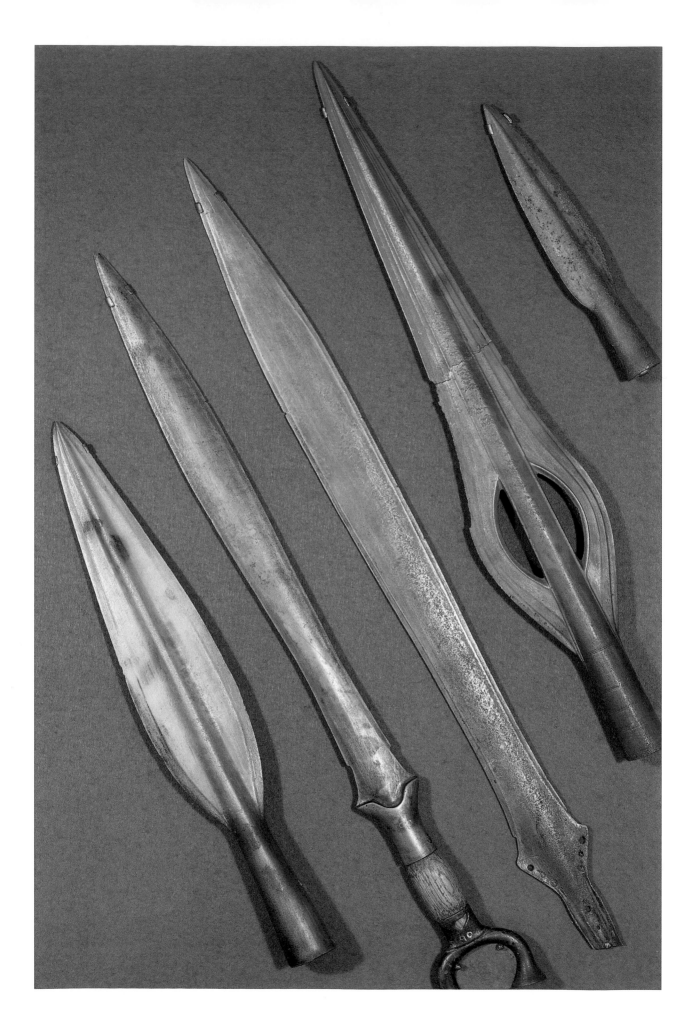

Weaponry

Swords

Most early commentators noted that the Celts had an unusual manner of fighting. Their chief weapon was a heavy, long-bladed sword, which they wielded with devastating efficiency. This type of weapon seems to have been developed to counteract the phalanx, the robust military formation that was favoured by the Greeks and other Mediterranean armies. Celtic warriors attempted to breach this solid mass of soldiers by making a ferocious frontal assault. Powerful weapons were essential if this kind of approach was to succeed and, judging by the rapid progress made during the period of Celtic expansion in the 4th century B.C., the tactic was effective for a time. Nonetheless, there were drawbacks. The initial

Bronze swords and spearheads from the Whittingham hoard, British, c. 600 B.C.

onslaught often resulted in high casualties and, if it failed, the impetus of the attack could peter out very quickly. Many ancient sources confirm this, reporting how the Celts could become totally disheartened, if they did not achieve an immediate breakthrough. In addition, the weight of the sword made it cumbersome to use, which proved a great disadvantage in hand-to-hand fighting.

In design terms, the size of the blade made a substantial hilt essential, and it was in this area that most of the decoration was concentrated. Handles could be inlaid with precious materials, such as ivory and amber, or else could be fashioned into the shape of a stylized human figure. The latter provided a remarkably functional alternative. The torso of the figure acted as the handgrip, secured on either side by projecting arms and legs, while the pommel was formed out of a fearsome head with bulging eyes.

Detail of bronze scabbard from grave 994, Hallstatt cemetery, 5th century B.C.

Bearing in mind the symbolic importance which Celtic warriors attached to the human head, it is quite possible that this motif was included as a kind of talisman. The starkest figures can be found on swords dating back to the 2nd century B.C. Later examples were often influenced by provincial Roman art. On these, the head is sometimes shown with hair, and the facial expression is generally more bland and naturalistic.

Scabbards

By and large, scabbards offered greater scope for decoration and the range of options was considerable. The best-known individual example is the proto-Celtic scabbard from grave 994 at Hallstatt. The images on this – soldiers, horsemen, and figures turning a wheel – have a narrative quality that is unusual in Celtic art. The stylized dragons at the chape (or point), however, are much more typical. In true Celtic fashion, they almost seem to slither up the edge of the scabbard.

Plant forms and stylized animals proved to be the most popular motifs throughout the La Tène era. During the Waldalgesheim period, in particular, craftsmen demonstrated a preference for flowing tendril patterns, running the full length of the scabbard. These were usually

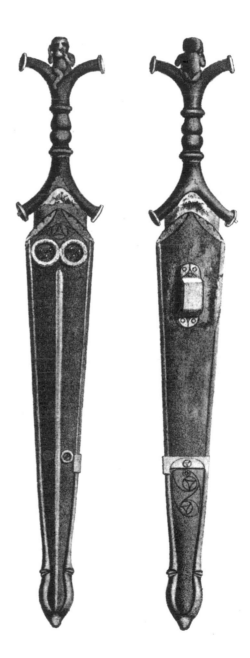

Daggers with anthropomorphic handles,
1st century B.C.

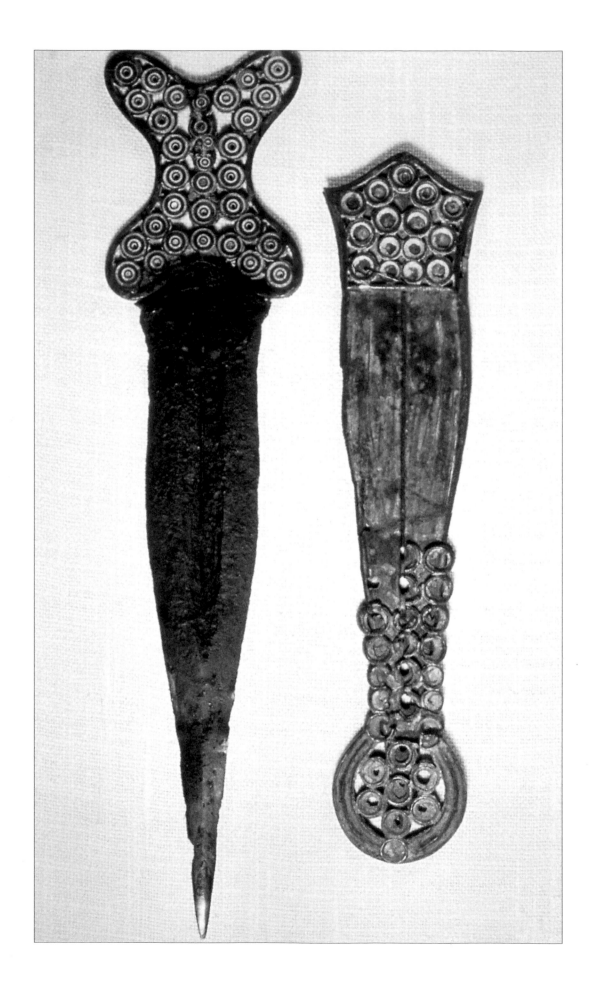

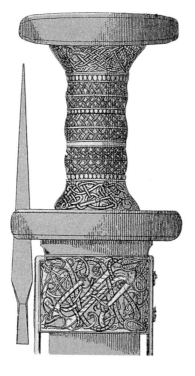

created with the aid of compasses. The tendril designs were often enlivened with faint hints of animal forms. On a French scabbard, discovered at Cernon-sur-Coole, eagle-eyed observers can discern a series of rudimentary bird heads. These consist of nothing more than a slit-like eye and a rapacious beak, which curves round sharply, merging with the line of the tendril.

Dragon pairs (S-shaped forms placed back to back) also figured on many scabbard patterns, dating back as far as the 4th century B.C.. Examples have been found throughout Celtic Europe, although the greatest concentrations were produced in Hungary and Switzerland. No fewer than six scabbards of this kind were discovered at the cemetery of Kosd, near Budapest. Some of these had been ritually damaged, before being cast onto the funeral pyre. In general, Swiss designs were less ostentatious and were frequently restricted to the area around the mouth of the scabbard. In addition to the usual methods of incising and hatching, their armourers also employed chagrinage or ring-punched decoration.

Similar designs can be observed on the surviving remnants of Celtic spears. These weapons were widely used at the start of the La Tène era and were invariably present in the earliest warrior graves. Indeed, the Gaesatae, one of the most warlike of the Celtic factions, are thought to have gained their name from the *gaesum*, a Gaulish throwing spear. In later periods, though, the influence of the weapon gradually began to diminish.

Iron and bronze dagger with sheath, British, 5th/4th century B.C.

Shields

Archaeologists have come across two distinct classes of arms and armour at Celtic sites. There are the functional items, often bearing the scars of battle, which were interred in warriors' graves. In addition, there are much more attractive articles, lavishly decorated and clearly never intended for practical use. These ceremonial pieces were placed in the graves of chieftains or other figures of exalted rank. Alternatively, they were donated to the gods as a form of sacrifice. Many of these items have been retrieved from rivers and lakes, where they were deliberately discarded. From an archaeological point of view, the advantage of this practice is that the artefacts have often survived in remarkably good condition. This is in marked contrast to the process of ritual damage, where objects were bent or broken prior to the sacrifice.

The splendour of much of this weaponry derives partly from the Celtic taste for ostentation, a fact that is confirmed in several classical sources, and partly from their reverential attitude to arms and armour. The finest pieces were thought to have distinctive personalities of their own. Reflecting this, the weapons of Celtic legend were often given names and had special powers attributed to them. Most people will have heard of King Arthur's sword, Excalibur, but this is only one example among many. In the early Irish epic, the *Táin Bó Cuailnge*, Fergus Mac Roth wielded a mighty sword called Cladcholg, which was powerful enough to slice through hilltops. Similarly, another character in the tale owned a shield called Ochain. This shrieked aloud whenever its master was in danger, and caused all the other shields in Ulster to scream in unison with it. Stories of this kind would have been familiar to many Celtic chieftains, who would doubtless have given personal names to their own weapons.

The shields used by Celtic warriors were quite different from their Mediterranean counterparts. The latter were normally round or curved, whilst the Celts preferred to use long, flat shields with a protruding central section. This could either take the form of a circular boss or a slender, rib-shaped umbo. The purpose of the cavity was to provide the warrior with a

Detail of central boss from Witham shield, British, 3rd century B.C.

The Battersea shield, from the River Thames in London, c. 1st century B.C.

more comfortable handgrip which, in turn, offered greater manoeuvrability. The drawback, however, was that the boss could endanger the wearer. In early La Tène models, it was only held in place by two nails, which could be pushed dangerously close to the warrior's hand, if the protrusion was struck with any force. In time, this led to the enlargement of the boss, so that the nails could be located further away from the hand or, alternatively, to the creation of a combined boss and rib cavity.

On most ceremonial items, the decoration was focused on this important central section. Craftsmen delighted in adding swirling La Tène designs to the circular boss, studding it with pieces of red glass or enamel. In a few instances, only the central boss has survived, suggesting that it may originally have been fixed onto a wooden or leather shield.

The most elaborate designs exploited the combination of the mid-rib and the boss. This is illustrated most persuasively on two British shields, which were dredged out of the River Witham and the River Thames. In both cases, the ends of the rib have been enlarged to form two extra bosses. These are purely ornamental, serving no practical purpose. On the Witham shield, the bosses were created with a mixture of delicate repoussé work and engraving. This was at its finest on the edges of the outer roundels, where the artist conjured up a subtle evocation of two long-snouted beasts, in the ambiguous manner which the Celts admired so much. The Witham shield has also attracted attention for another reason. Tiny rivet holes indicate that it once bore an entirely different design, which was removed by a later owner. The original pattern was a primitive representation of a boar with spindly, stilt-like legs. This was apt, since the boar was a conventional war symbol, but it is equally clear why the new owner replaced it with the sinuous elegance of the current design. The change is also interesting, because it confirms that Celtic warlords liked to personalize their equipment, just as the knights of a later age would do through the medium of heraldry.

On the Battersea shield, the same format has been taken a stage further. The mid-rib has effectively disappeared and the three roundels have expanded to cover much of the shield surface. The boss surrounding the handgrip – the only functional element in the design – forms just a small part of the central roundel. Around it, the craftsman has constructed a fluid, curvilinear pattern, consisting mostly of interlocking S-shapes and spirals. This theme is continued in the coloured enamel inlays, which feature a number of tiny swastikas. These rotate in a clockwise direction and can be classed as angular spirals. Apart from their obvious elegance, spirals also offered artists the opportunity to create playful hints of figuration. If you look at the shield from different angles, faces seem to appear. In the central roundel, for example, it is possible to make out stylized birds' heads, while the spirals which connect the roundels have been interpreted either as bulls with extravagantly curved horns or men with flowing moustaches.

Helmets

There is no doubt that the Battersea shield was conceived purely as a luxury item. Originally, it was gilded and, almost certainly, it was deposited in the Thames as a votive offering. This trend was echoed in the production of helmets, where the use of precious materials and showy designs was even more widespread.

The most lavish Celtic helmets were those created in the 'jockey-cap' format. These were inspired by Etruscan or Italian models and date back to around the 4th century B.C. In most cases, they consist of a hemispherical cap, a hinged cheek-flap, a neck-guard, and a fitting at the top for a plume or crest. Bands of decoration cover the entire surface, which may also be studded with pieces of coral or coloured glass.

The most spectacular example is the Agris helmet, which was discovered in a grotto near Angoulême in 1981. The crown itself is iron, but the attachments are made of bronze, covered in gold leaf, and the rivets are silver. The bands of decoration have a transitional flavour, blending elements from the Early and Waldalgesheim Styles. Geometric patterns nestle alongside running palmette and lotus motifs. The sinuous decoration

Jockey-cap helmet from Amfreville, France, 4th century B.C.

on the one surviving cheek-piece is particularly interesting, as it appears to represent a horned serpent. This was a conventional chthonian symbol, which implies that the grotto may have been revered as an entrance to the Celtic Otherworld.

The style of this piece is not far removed from another French helmet of similar date, which was discovered at Amfreville-sous-les-Monts. In this case, the helmet was retrieved from the dried-out bed of a tributary of the Seine, which suggests that it may have been used as a traditional votive offering. Here, only the central band is covered in gold leaf, though its pattern is considerably more refined than the Agris model. It consists of a linked arrangement of triskeles (three-coiled spirals), interspersed with elongated S-curves. The outer bands feature openwork decoration, inlaid with nuggets of coloured glass.

Horned helmet, found in the Thames near Waterloo Bridge, London, 1st century B.C.

Another notable jockey-cap helmet was discovered in 1895, in a tomb complex at Canosa di Puglia. Despite its Italian location, this, too, was probably made in Gaul and perhaps belonged to a Celtic mercenary. In this case, there is no gold leaf at all. Instead, the openwork design of lyres and S-curves is set with pieces of coral. Comparisons have often been drawn between this and the painted decoration on the Prunay vase, which dates from the same period.

In other Gaulish helmets, the surface design was generally less ornate, but the overall shape was often more elaborate. This is particularly true of the lofty, pointed helmets, which have been discovered in the Marne region. Several

historians have noted the similarity between their distinctive silhouette and contemporary Persian helmets, suggesting that the influence may have been transmitted through Italy, but it is equally possible that the style developed independently in Gaul. The two most celebrated examples come from warrior graves at Berru and La Gorge Meillet. In both cases, the decoration takes the form of incised motifs, such as swastikas and palmettes, and vacant discs which probably once contained pieces of coral. Although not as lavish as the 'jockey-caps', these helmets were certainly produced for figures of high standing. The warrior at La Gorge Meillet was interred with full military regalia and an Otherworld feast. The remains of his charioteer were buried above him.

Across the Channel, the nearest equivalent is the Waterloo Bridge helmet, which was discovered in the River Thames. This is considerably later, dating from around the 1st century B.C., and it displays a sparse, asymmetrical pattern of winding tendrils. Its most

Bronze helmet from La Gorge Meillet, France, 5th century B.C.

interesting features are the horns, which are studded with ornamental rivets. Horns symbolized virility and aggression, making them the ideal adornment for a war helmet.

War Trumpets

Classical authors often commented on the terrible din which Celtic warriors made when they went into battle. Much of this was accomplished through a combination of shouts, boasts and taunts, but the Celts also made use of ear-shattering war horns. Writers such as Polybius and Diodorus Siculus described the instrument as a *carnyx*, a Greek word for an animal-headed trumpet. Depictions of it can be found on the Roman arch at Orange, in the south of France, where it was pictured along with

Detail of Gundestrup cauldron with boar-headed trumpets on right.

other items of local booty. More interestingly, it is also shown on one of the plates of the Gundestrup Cauldron. There, the instruments are carried aloft by a group of warriors. Each one consists of a long-stemmed horn, crowned by the head of an open-mouthed boar. The latter was a traditional symbol of war and, fittingly, several of the warriors on the cauldron were portrayed with boar-crests on their helmets.

Findings of an actual carnyx are rare. Sir Joseph Banks, the famous naturalist, owned one but destroyed it accidentally, in an ill-advised attempt to analyse its metal. Fortunately, however, substantial remains of another carnyx were unearthed by peat-cutters at Deskford in Scotland. This example is made of beaten bronze and probably dates from the 1st century A.D. At the time of its discovery in 1874, the boar's head still retained its enamelled eyes and movable wooden tongue, though these have since disappeared.

Horse Trappings

Horses and chariots played an integral role in the martial activities of the Celts. Accordingly, warrior chieftains took pains to deck them out with the kind of finery that would set off their own ceremonial gear. Horse-bits, harness mounts and terrets (chariot rings) were all adorned with the full repertoire of Celtic motifs. Many examples of these have been found in the cart or chariot burials, which date back as far as the Hallstatt period. In these, persons of high rank were interred along with the vehicle. In most cases, the chariot was dismantled and, on rare occasions, the owner's horses were sacrificed and placed inside the grave.

There are enormous regional variations in the style of decoration employed on these accoutrements. Some of the most sumptuous chariot graves were discovered in the Marne region in France, where there was a pronounced taste for openwork phalerae (bronze discs), decorated with enamel. The example from the tomb at Cuperly (4th century B.C.), meticulously designed with the aid of compasses, is particularly fine. Phalerae were normally used as harness fittings, although they might occasionally be fixed to a warrior's armour.

Bronze harness mounts from the Roman fort at South Shields, England, late 2nd century A.D.

The items found at the chariot grave of Mezek, in Bulgaria, could hardly be more different. These include a range of yoke mounts, terrets and linchpins, which are prime examples of the Plastic Style. Knobbed protruberances jut out at every angle, hinting at swollen-cheeked faces and bulging eyes.

In Britain, by contrast, the preference was for brightly coloured enamel mounts, which made use of the latest champlevé techniques. Here, the principal finds

Cruciform harness-trapping in bronze enamel, 1st century A.D.

were made at Polden Hill in Somerset, where a sizeable hoard of mounts and fittings was uncovered by a ploughman in 1803, and at Stanton in Norfolk.

Bronze harness-trapping from the Polden Hill hoard, England, 1st century A.D.

A few items relate specifically to horses. Depictions of the animal are surprisingly rare, but one of the most charming is a tiny chariot mount, which was discovered at Melsonby in Yorkshire, among a hoard of artefacts buried by the Brigantes. The horse's face is conveyed by a few simple curves, an example of Celtic stylization at its finest. More unusual still is the bronze pony cap, which was extracted from a bog at Torrs in Scotland. The cap once belonged to the novelist, Sir Walter Scott, and it features a repoussé design with spiral and bird's head motifs.

Detail of the Gundestrup vessel, showing a dead warrior being lowered into a cauldron

Ritual Objects

Cauldrons

Cauldrons featured prominently in the everyday lives of many prehistoric peoples. In essence, they were large feasting vessels, which could be used for boiling meat or heating drink. Often, they were huge. Fragments from some of the larger finds suggest a capacity of over 600 litres. In addition, cauldrons were sometimes employed as cremation vessels. The Urnfield people, for example, placed the ashes of their dead in them in the course of their wagon burials.

The Celts certainly used cauldrons both for feasting and for some funerary rites, but the vessel swiftly acquired a range of other, near-magical associations. In Irish lore, they were symbols of abundance. Each of the feasting halls in the Otherworld contained its own cauldron, which produced inexhaustible supplies of food. Goibhniu, the craft-god, filled his with a special brew which made the drinker immortal, while Daghda, the

Irish father-god, owned a vessel so enormous that it could satisfy any appetite.

Cauldrons were also linked with death and regeneration. In Welsh myth, King Matholwch possessed a magic vessel which could restore slain warriors to life. If a dead soldier was cooked in it overnight, he would awaken the next day hale and hearty, save for the fact that he had lost the power of speech. This tale is particularly interesting, because it appears to echo a detail on one of the plates of the Gundestrup cauldron. The scene in question shows a corpse being held upside-down by a giant, presumably a deity, and lowered into a large vessel.

In later Celtic lore, there was an increasing tendency for stories about magic cauldrons to overlap with the legend of the Holy Grail. In one such tale, for example, King Arthur embarked on a quest to find a fabulous cauldron, encrusted with diamonds. This vessel, it transpired, could only be heated by the breath of nine virgins and would never cook meat for a coward. Similarly, Taliesin, the semi-mythical bard, gained the power of prophecy after drinking from a 'cauldron of science and inspiration' while, in the Middle Ages, the Virgin Mary herself was sometimes described as a 'cauldron of inspiration'.

The sheer persistence of such legends illustrates the powerful associations that cauldrons carried in Celtic eyes. Their significance is further confirmed by a wealth of archaeological evidence. In the Hallstatt era, cauldrons were occasionally placed in burial chambers, to provide posthumous sustenance for the deceased. In the tumulus of Eberdingen-Hochdorf, for example, an ornamental vessel filled with mead was left close to the body of the dead prince. More often, cauldrons were linked with votive offerings at holy sites. At Duchcov in central Europe, for instance, archaeologists unearthed a massive vessel containing more than 2000 items of jewellery, which had been deposited near a sacred spring. In other cases, the cauldron itself provided the offering. Some of the finest surviving remains have been discovered in Denmark and northern Germany, where they were deliberately abandoned at watery shrines.

The outstanding find in this field is the Gundestrup cauldron. This enigmatic piece came to light in 1891, at the Raevemose peat bog in Jutland. It is made of solid silver and consists of 13 separate plates. These were originally covered in a thin layer of gold foil. One of them formed the base of the vessel, while the remainder were arranged around the inner and outer surfaces of the bowl. Each of the plates is decorated with a profusion of animal and mythological scenes. These plates were dismantled and placed inside the vessel, before it was deposited in the marsh. Pollen analysis confirms that it was placed on a dry piece of earth, rather than buried. Since, presumably, it was in plain view, the sanctity of the place must have been considerable, to discourage thieves from removing such a precious object.

The Gundestrup cauldron is, without doubt, the most splendid and also the most controversial of all Celtic treasures. Estimates of its date and its true origins vary wildly, and some authorities even question whether it can genuinely be described as Celtic. Indeed, the only general point of agreement is that the cauldron was not made in Denmark. The most popular theory is that it was created by Thracian silversmiths, in the region of present-day Romania or Bulgaria. The style of the workmanship, the technique of using silver embossed in high relief, and the portrayal of some of the animals all lend weight to this view. On the other hand, the nature of

The Gundestrup cauldron, discovered in a Danish peat bog, c. 1st century B.C.

the cauldron itself and the iconography of some of the scenes are distinctly Celtic, and have no parallels in Thracian art. Rather, they point to Gaulish origins. Neither of these factors, however, explain how the cauldron came to Denmark. Many suggestions have been mooted. Some believe that it was brought there by German mercenaries attached to the Roman army; others that it was part of the booty looted from Gaul; while yet another authority maintains that it was made by the Scordisci tribe, who settled for a time in Thracian territory, and that it was carried to the west by raiders from the Cimbri people.

The imagery on the plates of the cauldron is highly ambiguous and has done nothing to resolve these questions. The seven outer plates depict the heads of impressive, torc-wearing characters, presumably deities, accompanied by a few tiny figures. The inner plates are crowded with smaller, narrative scenes. Among these, there are two images which have aroused particular interest in Celtic circles. The first of these shows a figure wearing antlers, sitting cross-legged on the ground. He wears a torc around his neck and, in his hands, he holds a second torc and a ram-horned snake. A medley of animals are clustered around him, including a boy riding on a dolphin.

This figure is usually identified as Cernunnos, the Celtic god of fertility and nature. His presence would explain the various creatures in the background, particularly the ram-horned serpent. The latter was a hybrid mythical beast, frequently portrayed on Celtic artefacts. It combined the fertility symbolism of the ram with the regenerative powers of the snake – an association stemming from the creature's ability to shed and renew its skin. By tradition, most Celtic gods were shown wearing torcs, the conventional emblems of rank and status. Where a second torc was depicted, this usually represented abundance, a quality which is entirely appropriate for Cernunnos.

Adjoining this scene, there is a second plate with strong Celtic associations. This portrays a procession of horsemen and foot soldiers. The latter are carrying the long shields with bosses, which Celtic warriors are known to have used, and they are accompanied by three figures blowing boar-headed trumpets. Above, some of the cavalrymen have boar-crests on their helmets, a well-documented feature of Celtic armour. To the left, a

Detail from Gundestrup cauldron depicting Cernunnos, the horned fertility god.

giant immerses a dead man in a large vessel. This is normally interpreted as an illustration of the resurrectionary powers of cauldrons, although there are some who see it as a human sacrifice to Teutates, the Celtic god of war. The victims who were offered up to this deity were usually drowned. Two other plates on the Gundestrup cauldron relate to the sacrifice of bulls, which was also commonplace among the Celts.

The rich decoration and complex symbolism of the Gundestrup cauldron are unique, but a number of other, less famous cauldrons can also be linked with La Tène artists. In 1952, the remnants of a bronze cauldron were discovered at Brå, in eastern Jutland. The vessel had been deliberately broken up, doubtless as a form of ritual damage, before being buried in a pit. Although considerably plainer than the Gundestrup cauldron, the Brå vessel was much larger, with a capacity of around 600 litres. Its main features are a series of bronze mounts, which were originally attached to the rim of the vessel. These include five bulls' heads and a vicious-looking

Fragment of a bronze cauldron from Rynkeby, Denmark, 1st century B.C.

owl mask, all of them fine examples of the Plastic Style of decoration. The cauldron is thought to have been made in Moravia. The bull motif was repeated on another damaged cauldron, which was discovered at Rynkeby on the Danish island of Funen.

Stonework and Carving

Given their preference for abstract or stylized forms, it is scarcely surprising that the Celts should have left us comparatively few images of their gods. Many of the finest surviving examples were carved out of stone, and placed in or near important burial sites.

Pride of place is usually given to depictions of Cernunnos, the horned-god, since he is the only deity that has been positively identified through an inscription. This was discovered on a rather worn altar relief, originally located beneath the present-day church of Notre-Dame de Paris. The monument was erected by Parisian sailors and was dedicated to Tiberius. On the strength of this, a number of other portrayals of the deity have been

Cernunnos with Apollo and Mercury, altar from Reims, France, 1st century A.D.

identified. The most notable of these is a Gallo-Roman altar from Reims, which shows Cernunnos sitting cross-legged between the figures of Apollo and Mercury. The sculpture dates from the 1st century A.D., after Gaul had been Romanized. This accounts for the overtly classical appearance of the group. Even so, several of the god's traditional attributes are clearly recognizable. These include his horns, the torc around his neck and the animals at his feet. In his lap, he holds a sack of money, which represents abundance. The rat above his head relates to the underworld and, in this instance, probably refers to Mercury rather than Cernunnos. The horned god was most popular in Gaul, although evidence of his worship has also been found elsewhere. On some of his shrines, the deity's antlers were removable. This implies that the rites associated with him may have been seasonal, coinciding with the natural growth of a stag's antlers.

After Cernunnos, the most widely represented deity was the horse-

Sandstone figure from Euffigneix,
France, 1st century B.C.

goddess, Epona. This may be due to the fact that, alone of all the Celtic divinities, she was worshipped at Rome. In most cases, Epona was shown riding side-saddle on a mare or, alternatively, standing between a pair of horses. On coins, she was occasionally represented as a horse with a woman's head. The goddess represented fertility, particularly in relation to horse-breeding, but she was also linked with death. On some images, she was portrayed with a key. One of her roles, it seems, was to conduct human souls to the Otherworld and the key symbolized her access to this legendary realm. Predictably, the cult of Epona was especially popular with cavalrymen. Her name is the source of the English word 'pony'.

Regrettably, many of the remaining images of Celtic gods can no longer be identified. Nevertheless, they can be classified under a number of different thematic groupings. It is noticeable, for example, that many Celtic deities had zoomorphic overtones. Cernunnos himself was often represented with cloven feet, and this tendency can be discerned in a variety of other figures. The tiny sandstone statue from Euffigneix in eastern Gaul is particularly striking. Measuring just over 25cm, it was probably intended for private devotions, rather than for a larger tribal shrine. The stylized face has been damaged but this is overshadowed, in any case, by the spirited depiction of a boar on the front of the figure. Its dorsal bristles are erect, an aggressive feature which normally underlined the creature's role as a war symbol. On one side of the statuette, there is also an outsized carving of a single human eye, its prominent eyebrow echoing the line of the boar's crest. No one has been able to find a satisfactory explanation for this combination of motifs, although the figure is sometimes thought to represent a hunting god.

Made of bronze rather than stone, the curious figure from Bouray falls into the same category. A cursory glance might suggest a classical source, but closer examination reveals not only the torc around the neck, but also the figure's awkward, squat-legged position. The tiny legs, which are out of proportion with the rest of the figure, resemble the hooves of a deer. Indeed, if it were not for the complete absence of antlers, it would be tempting to interpret this as a depiction of Cernunnos. The figure was dredged out of the River Juine, to the south of Paris, in 1845. It was fashioned out of sheet metal, and it seems quite possible that its designer

was a specialist cauldron-maker. Certainly, there are some stylistic affinities with the figures on the cauldron from Rynkeby.

Many of the other worthies represented by Celtic stonemasons take the form of pillar-statues. This reflects their original purpose, which was to crown the summits of ancient burial mounds. One of the oldest discoveries in this vein was the life-sized figure of a warrior, carved out of sandstone, which was found near the German tomb of Hirschlanden. The statue dates back to the 6th century B.C. and was originally placed at the top of the barrow, until it was broken off at the feet. Its various attributes – the conical helmet, the weighty neck-ring, the dagger hanging from a belt, and the erect phallus – were all designed to emphasize the heroic status of the princeling in the tomb below. The distorted facial features are sometimes thought to represent a mask.

The stone monuments at other Celtic burial places offer variants on this theme. At Pfalzfeld in the Rhineland, the stele takes the form of a tapering, four-sided pillar. This was decorated with a series of stylized human faces, each with a leaf-crown headdress and a lotus-bud carved on its forehead. The emphasis on various plant forms suggests that the pillar may have been intended as a representation of a sacred tree. The shaft of the pillar is broken at the top, and it is likely that it was once surmounted by a larger version of the stylized heads.

Janiform figures provided an alternative format for the pillar-statue. With their ability to gaze out in two directions at once, Janus heads were particularly appropriate for the tops of tumuli, dominating their entire surroundings. The best surviving example is a sandstone pillar-statue from Holzerlingen. This is slightly more than life-sized and shows Celtic stylization at its most severe. The mouth is nothing more than a horizontal gash and the heavy, hooded eyes exude menace. Unlike the Hirschlanden figure, which was meant to glorify the occupant of the tomb, this is clearly a deity of some kind. By tradition, Janus figures fulfilled a protective, custodial function, and this may well have been the intention here.

Bronze statue of a Celtic deity from Bouray,
France, 1st century B.C./1st century A.D.

Originally, there was a horn-shaped protrusion between the heads. It is not clear whether this was a variant of the leaf crown, as seen on the Pfalzfeld pillar, or whether the deity was actually horned.

Smaller janiform figures have also been unearthed at the Gaulish shrine of Roquepertuse, in Provence. Here, the finds consist solely of heads and there can be no doubt about their watchful purpose. They were designed to be placed over a doorway or entrance. This is confirmed by the fact that there is no modelling on the sides of the sculpture, emphasizing that it was never meant to be seen from that angle. At an early stage, the heads were painted and, as is so often the case with Janus heads, the two faces are different. The frown on one of them is rather more intense than the other.

The sanctuary at Roquepertuse was thoroughly excavated in the 1920s, offering a rare insight into Celtic ritual practices. It may date from as early as the 6th century B.C. and it was in continuous use for several centuries, until it was destroyed by fire at the start of the 2nd century B.C. At the entrance to the shrine, there was a portico consisting of three limestone pillars. These contained niches, where the skulls of defeated enemies were triumphantly displayed. Similar activities were carried out at Entremont, another Provençal retreat. This featured the same arrangement of severed heads, nailed into cavities in pillars, but at Entremont there were also a number of carvings of these grisly trophies. On these, the faces had no mouths and were shown with their eyes closed, pointing to the fact that they were dead.

At Roquepertuse, archaeologists also made a number of other discoveries: a series of carved birds, a crudely executed frieze of horses, damaged statues of two cross-legged figures, and traces of animal paintings. Originally, there were five statues, perhaps mounted on pedestals. The remaining pair have lost their heads and arms, making it hard to determine their initial purpose. It is likely that they represented either heroic soldiers or war gods. Sections of armour can still be discerned at the top of the torsos and, like the Janus heads, the figures were once coloured. It has also been suggested that the missing hands may once have presented severed heads towards the spectator. This theory is based on comparisons with the Tarasque de Noves, a chilling sculpture which portrays a ravening monster, probably a form of lion, holding two severed heads beneath its paws. From

Stone figure of Janus-heads from Roquepertuse, France, 3rd century B.C.

Portico with severed heads from the shrine of Roquepertuse, 3rd century B.C.

its jaws, a human arm dangles lifelessly. A similar creature was found at Linsdorf, in Alsace. In both cases, the inspiration is thought to have come from classical funerary art. The Romans often used scenes of animals devouring humans in this context, to symbolize the triumph of death.

Votive Figures

Comparatively little wood-carving has come down to us from the Celtic era, largely because of the perishable nature of the material. The majority of the surviving pieces are votive figures, which were cast into the water at sacred springs or river shrines. Unlike the magnificent weapons and items of jewellery that were discarded at other sites, these wooden figurines were usually plain, cheaply made objects. They were also deposited for a very specific purpose, namely to invoke the healing powers of tutelary deities.

The most important healing shrines that have come to light are both in France, at Chamalières in the Massif Central and at Sources-de-la-Seine near Dijon. The latter was dedicated to Sequana, the personification of the River Seine. Between them, these two sites have yielded up several thousand votive offerings. In general, the sacrificed items appeared in two main guises. Often, they took the form of the limb or organ that was diseased. In other words, the supplicant might offer up a wooden image of a damaged hand in the hope that, in exchange, the deity would restore their real hand to health.

The second type of offering was the so-called 'pilgrim' figure, representing the actual donor. These ranged from fairly naturalistic pieces, frequently betraying the influence of classical art, to stylized, armless figures, wearing thick, hooded cloaks. Their appearance is reminiscent of the Cucullati, the hooded deities who were worshipped in many parts of the Celtic world.

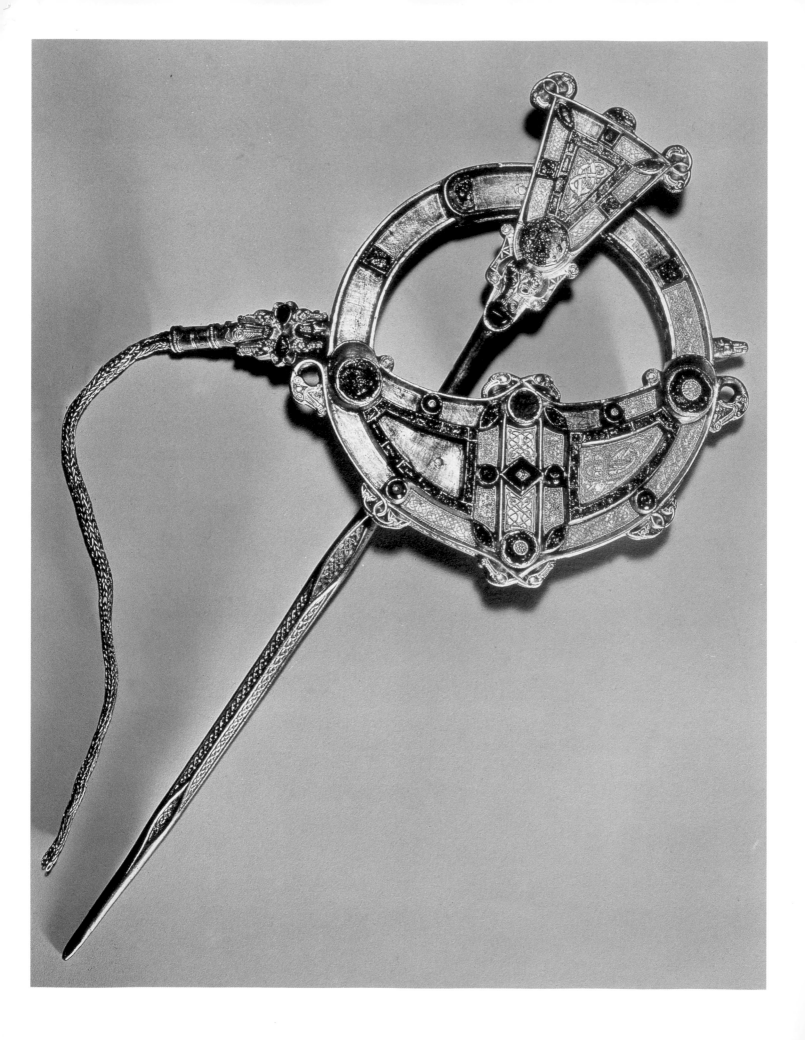

Jewellery

Torcs

The Celts' passion for golden trinkets and fine jewellery is well documented. Classical authors talked with ill-concealed cupidity about the riches of *'Gallia aurifera'* (gold-bearing Gaul), while still implying that it created a dangerous flaw in the psyche of its people. Strabo, for example, wrote scathingly about their 'childish boastfulness and love of decoration. They wear ornaments of gold, torcs on their necks, and bracelets on their arms and wrists, and their nobles adorn themselves with dyed garments sprinkled with gold. It is this vanity which makes them so unbearable in victory and so downcast in defeat ...'

The most prestigious item of jewellery was the torc. This was a heavy metal collar, probably of Eastern origin, which fulfilled a number of

The Tara brooch, Ireland, 8th century A.D.

FOLLOWING PAGES Gold torc from the tomb of the princess of Vix, France, 6th century B.C.

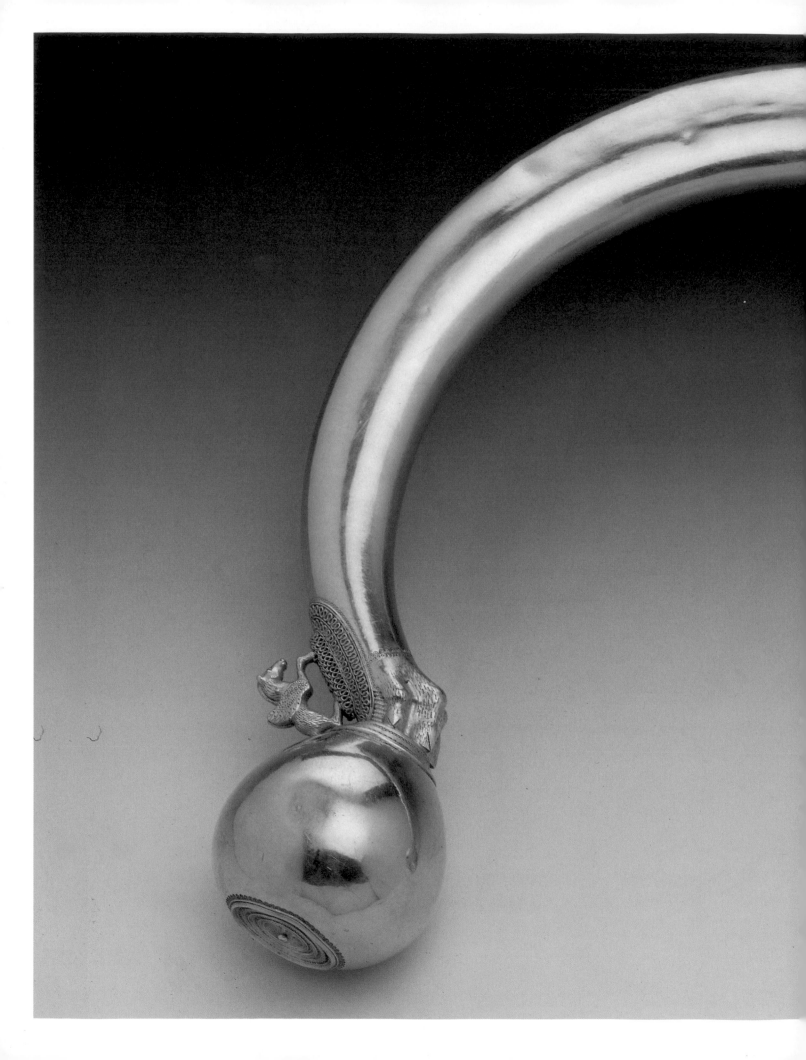

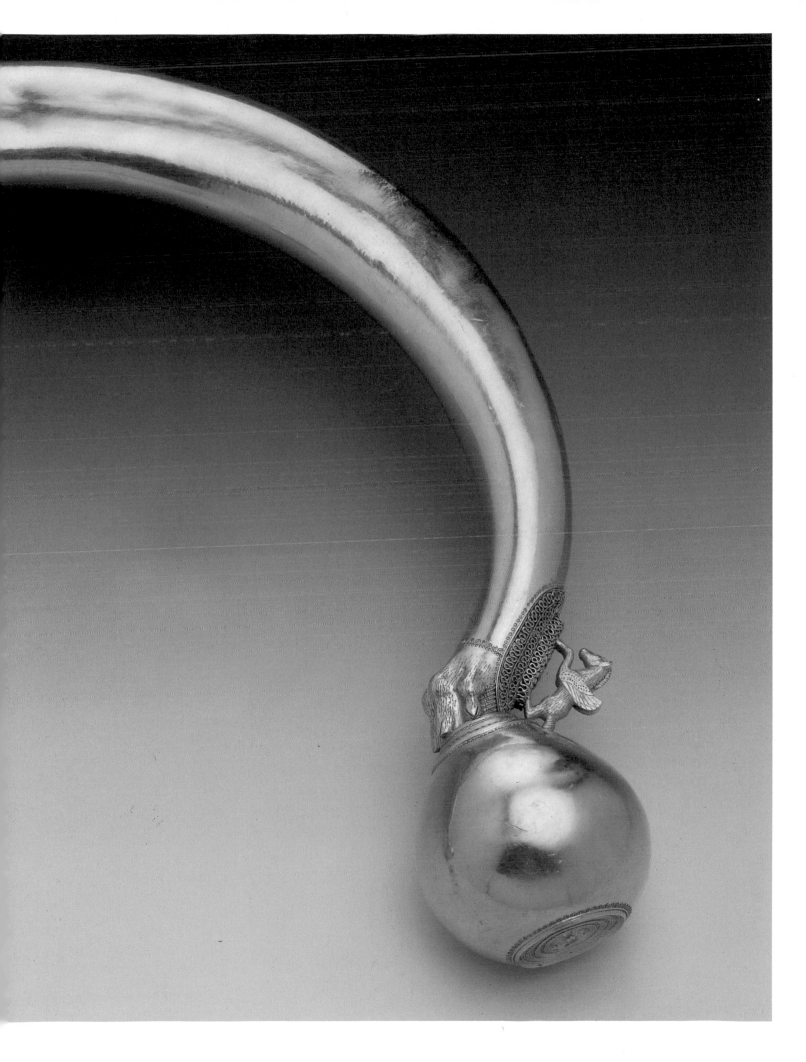

functions in Celtic society. Among the princes and chieftains, it was a sign of wealth and status. Lavish examples have been found in early Hallstatt and La Tène burial sites, particularly in female graves. This may mean that fathers passed their torcs down directly to their sons, perhaps as a badge of leadership.

Torcs also had strong ritual associations. Celtic deities were invariably shown wearing or holding them, as the images on the Gundestrup cauldron and surviving stone-carvings confirm, and they were often used as votive offerings. Further hints of their supernatural powers can be found in *The Cattle Raid of Cooley*, an early Irish epic, where Morann the Arbiter wore a magical torc, which tightened around his neck whenever he gave a false judgement. In a martial context, torcs were thought to act like talismans, offering the wearer some mystical form of protection. Classical sources recorded with astonishment how some Celtic warriors would go naked into battle, bearing only their weapons and a torc around their neck.

In decorative terms, the torc was highly versatile. It was pliant enough to be pulled open, but sufficiently robust to take ornamentation over its entire surface. It could also be made in a variety of different sizes and materials. Indeed, some torcs were so large and heavy that they can only have been worn very rarely, on ceremonial occasions.

Perhaps the most sumptuous of the surviving torcs is the magnificent item which was buried with the princess of Vix. This is made of 96 percent pure gold and weighs some 480g. The decoration, as it is so often with torcs, is focused on the terminals. These take the form of two large globes, attached to lions' paws. In addition, there are two tiny winged horses, mounted on beds of golden filigree. Given its early date (6th century B.C.), the technical sophistication of the piece is remarkable. It consists of 20 separate components, some of them cast (the Pegasus figures, the paws) and some beaten out (the hollow spheres). Parts of the decoration were punched from the interior of the object, and the remaining elements were then soldered together.

Of course, not all torcs were this lavish. The celebrated example found at Trichtingen, in southern Germany, was made of far less costly materials, but it was still deemed sufficiently fine to be cast into a pool as a votive offering. The torc is made of silver-plated iron and has an Eastern flavour, which suggests that it was produced in the lower Danube area. Its most intriguing features, however, are the two short-horned bulls, which constitute the terminals. The motif of confronted animal heads was extremely popular with Celtic craftsmen, and echoes of it can be seen in the border decoration of many, later manuscripts. Here, there is added

Torc from the Snettisham hoard, England, 1st century B.C.

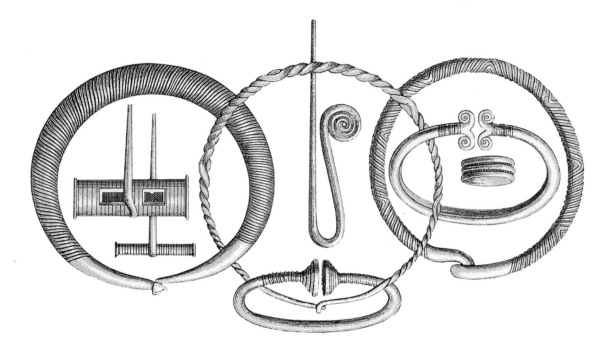

interest in the fact that the bulls themselves are wearing torcs. This
suggests that the piece may have had links with the cult of bull-worship,
which was common in many parts of the Celtic world.

More than most other artefacts from the La Tène period, the torc was
prey to dramatic regional variations. In the Champagne area of France, for
example, early neck-rings displayed the usual emphasis on the terminals,
which were generally either triangular or torus-shaped, before local
craftsmen developed an entirely different format. This was the ternary torc,
so-called because the hoop was decorated with three, identical protrusions.
The band itself was sometimes adorned with an engraved leaf-pattern.

Across the Channel, the principal finds occurred at Snettisham in
Norfolk and Broighter in Co. Derry. The Snettisham hoard was sizeable,
consisting of no fewer than 61 torcs. The finest of these were composed of
twisted strands of gold, with hooped ends and curvilinear reliefs. The
Broighter collar was part of a smaller hoard, discovered by the shore of
Lough Foyle in 1896. Its hollow, tubular form is similar to some continental
models, but the sinuous ornamentation is typically Irish and has
sometimes been compared to the decoration on the Turoe stone.

Brooches

If torcs were the most exalted forms of personal adornment among the Celts, then brooches were the most popular. They were worn by both men and women, and they served a variety of purposes. On a purely practical level, they often acted as clothes-fasteners while, at other times, they carried talismanic overtones or were valued for their decorative appeal.

As objects, they came in a bewildering diversity of guises though, in most cases, the ultimate inspiration was drawn from the classical world. This was certainly true of the two most basic forms of brooch, the hand pin and the fibula. By and large, pins were long and slender with finely decorated heads. These usually consisted of metal beading or *millefiori* enamel studs.

The fibula, on the other hand, offered more scope for invention. In essence, it resembled a kind of safety-pin, dating back to Mycenaean times. From as early as the 5th century B.C., however, Celtic craftsmen began to toy with this simple, S-shaped design. They expanded the bow, partly for practical reasons – so that it could be used to fasten a more substantial piece of material – and partly as a matter of aesthetics. For, the pronounced arch of the fibula made it an ideal setting for the sinuous curves of the La Tène style.

The most striking examples tended to take the form of fantastic animals or stylized humans. These are generally known as 'mask' fibulae. The richest finds have occurred in Germany and Central Europe, the finest of all, perhaps, being the Parsberg brooch, which was discovered in a grave in the Rhineland. This extraordinary piece has a stylized human head at either end of its S-curve. Both have bulging eyes, a prominent

Celtic silver-gilt brooch from Birdlip,
1st century A.D.

nose and no mouth, and the lower figure also sports a set of pointed ears and a strange, conical hair-piece. Below him, the catchplate of the brooch takes the form of two skimpy griffins. Double-headed brooches of this kind were not unusual, and the effect was enhanced by the Celtic practice of wearing fibulae in pairs, linked together by a metal chain.

In Britain and Ireland, a very different type of brooch became popular. This was the penannular brooch, so-called because it had a small gap in its hoop which made it not quite annular. There is a measure of disagreement about its origins. Some believe that it evolved from provincial Roman models, while others argue that the basic design was native to Britain and had survived virtually unaltered since the Iron Age.

In its simplest form, the penannular brooch resembles a miniature torc – a simple hoop with the addition of a swivelling pin. During the Christian period, however, the ornamentation became much more elaborate. The head of the pin expanded into a kite-shaped panel and was often inlaid with tiny jewels. In addition, the terminals of the hoop became enlarged, forming a much thicker curve than the upper part of the ring. In some cases, the ring was closed completely and the brooch could only be attached to the owner's garments by means of the pin. Technically speaking, this is a pseudo-penannular brooch.

The two most famous Insular brooches are both pseudo-penannulars. The Hunterston brooch was found in Ayrshire, Scotland, although runic inscriptions on the reverse confirm that it once belonged to a Viking. The jewel probably dates back to the 8th century A.D., as does the more celebrated Tara brooch. Despite its name, this was actually found on the beach at Bettystown, Co. Meath, in 1850. According to popular lore, it was found in a wooden box by a group of children. Their mother sold it for a pittance to a watchmaker, who in turn sold it on to George Waterhouse, a Dublin jeweller. He gave the brooch its romantic name and arranged for it to be shown at the Great Exhibition of 1851.

The Salle brooch, England, 6th century A.D.

Detail of interlacing and animal decoration on the Tara brooch.

After this, its fame was assured and Waterhouse wasted no time in marketing facsimiles of the jewel.

Fortunately, the Tara brooch was worthy of its reputation. It is richly decorated on both sides, which suggests that it must have been made for a genuine connoisseur, since only the front would have been visible when in use. These surfaces are divided into a series of tiny panels, featuring a combination of engraved curvilinear patterns and filigree interlacing. Pieces of coloured glass, amber and granules of gold also punctuate the design. In addition, there are miniature ornaments projecting from the edges of the ring and the pinhead. These depict long-snouted beasts and fishtails and, in many ways, they resemble the border decoration in manuscripts like the *Lindisfarne Gospels* and the *Book of Kells*.

Other Items

Torcs and brooches were the most distinctive forms of jewellery produced by the Celts, although they did produce a range of other artefacts. Armlets, bracelets and ankle-rings were available throughout the La Tène era, and were frequently worn in matching pairs. Sometimes animal motifs were employed – snake-like bracelets appear to have been particularly popular – but the most eye-catching designs feature abstract or semi-abstract elements. The anklets from Klettham in Bavaria and from Planany in Bohemia, for instance, are fine examples of the enigmatic Plastic Style. Their knobbed protruberances, which were probably meant to be imitations of coral beads, actually help to create a typically Celtic sense of ambiguity. When viewed at certain angles, they resemble swollen, distorted faces with popping eyes.

Celtic craftsmen also liked to make a feature of clasps and buckles. Here, some of the most attractive examples date right back to the dawn of the La Tène period. They include an elegant series of belt-plaques and hooks with symmetrical, openwork designs. Exotic sphinxes and winged griffins figure prominently among the decoration, underlining the oriental influences which shaped the so-called Early Style. It may be misleading to think of all

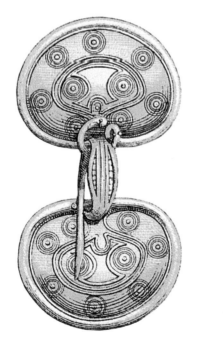

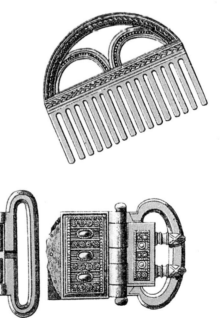

of these belt-hooks as jewellery, however, for some were used as clasps for carrying arms and should properly be classed as part of a warrior's equipment.

A few other artefacts are more commonly associated with jewellery. These include mirrors and combs, which often featured delicately engraved designs. The taste for the former was acquired from the classical world and, in particular, from the Etruscans. Celtic craftsmen mimicked their characteristic kidney shape, but adorned the backs with typical La Tène motifs. These took the form of tendril-like swathes of basketry patterns. Bronze mirrors were especially popular in Britain, with the finest examples originating from Desborough in Northamptonshire and Birdlip in Gloucestershire.

PREVIOUS PAGES *Bracelets and earrings from the tomb of the Princess of Vix, France, 6th century B.C.*

BELOW *Items of jewellery in the distinctive Plastic Style.*

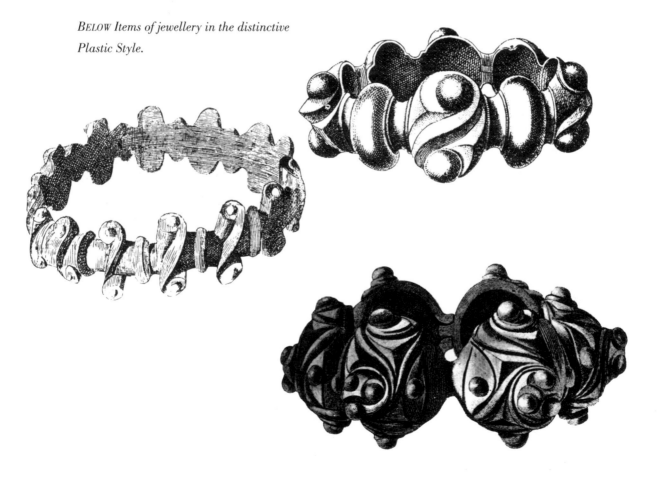

Bronze mirror from Desborough, England, 1st century B.C.

Symbol of St. Matthew, Echternach Gospels, late 7th century.

The Christian Contribution

The coming of Christianity opened up a new chapter in Celtic art. Unlike the Romans, who imposed their styles and institutions on the Celts of continental Europe, Christian missionaries took pains to adapt elements of local culture wherever possible. Accordingly, the old La Tène traditions, which still survived on the western fringes of the continent, received a new lease of life. Christian artists made extensive use of them, when creating artworks that would promote their faith. These fell into three broad categories: manuscripts of sacred texts, various items of liturgical equipment, and the stonework decoration on crosses and other Christian monuments.

Manuscripts

It is ironic, perhaps, that a people who had abjured the practice of writing for so long, should have made such a significant contribution to the art of book decoration. This was in itself a comparatively new field. The book or codex gradually began to replace papyrus as the chief writing material in the 3rd and 4th centuries A.D., and Insular artists were among the first to recognize its true potential.

The rise of the book coincided with the spread of Christianity, and many of the early texts were produced specifically to aid in the process of conversion. In the Celtic areas of western Europe, the most important kind of text was the Gospel Book. This came in a number of different formats. There were the portable versions, the so-called 'Pocket Gospels', which missionaries carried with them on their evangelical expeditions; there were the scholarly editions, which were used for study and research in monastic libraries; and there were the lavishly illustrated examples, complete with full-page illuminations and decorative calligraphy. These were designed to be seen rather than read. In most cases, they were either on open view on the high altar, or displayed during feast days and special processions.

Gospel Books contained a certain amount of prefatory material, followed by the four Gospels. The introductory matter would often include a prologue by St Jerome relating to the text. This reflected the longstanding dispute that was taking place within the Celtic Church. There was, as yet, no universally accepted translation of the Bible. Rome encouraged the use of the Vulgate, the translation which Pope Damasus had commissioned from St Jerome and which was completed in c.404. This version was widely used in the areas of Britain which had been converted by Roman missionaries. Elsewhere, however, there was still a tendency to use the less reliable 'Old Latin' translation. This was one of the many issues which the Synod of Whitby (664) sought to resolve. Occasionally, these differences are apparent from the illustrations in the Gospel Books. It is noticeable, for example, that the figure who represents St Matthew in the *Echternach Gospels* sports a Roman tonsure, while his counterpart in the *Book of Durrow* wears his hair in the Irish manner.

The remainder of the introductory section dealt with the arrangement of the Gospels themselves. At this stage, the verse and chapter divisions of the

Portrait of St John, MacDurnan Gospels, 9th century.

Bible had not yet been devised, making it hard for monks and priests to find their way around the text. Early Christian scholars tackled this problem in several ways, producing a variety of synopses and indexes. The most influential of these were the Canon Tables, which divided the text into numbered sections and enabled the reader to cross-refer from one Gospel to the next. The system was invented in the early 4th century by Eusebius of Caesarea, the biographer and personal adviser of Emperor Constantine. From an early date, these Canon Tables were presented in attractively painted arcades, becoming one of the focal points of the manuscript.

The technical capabilities of the Celtic illuminators advanced rapidly and, by the late 7th century, the decoration of the Gospel Books had reached a highly sophisticated level. The keys to this rapid progress were flexibility and eclecticism. Celtic artists drew their inspiration from a wealth of different sources and fused them imaginatively, to create an entirely new style. The sources in question included manuscripts from the Late Antique period, the curvilinear decoration on La Tène metalwork and stonework, and a variety of eastern influences, many of which were transmitted through contacts with Rome.

From the artists of Late Antiquity, the Celts borrowed the format of two of the standard forms of illustration in the Gospel Books. The Canon Tables, as mentioned, were traditionally displayed in an architectural setting, with the references from the Gospels listed between a series of columns. In addition, they adopted the notion of prefacing each of the Gospels with a portrait of the relevant Evangelist. Ultimately, this type of picture derived from classical author portraits, where a writer was shown working on his text. Usually, the author was seated in a room or in a niche, and he was often accompanied by a portrayal of his muse. The Celts, with their preference for abstract or stylized forms, found it hard to reproduce the illusionistic naturalism of either the architecture or the human figures. Instead, they flattened out the forms and rendered them in a semi-

Decorative calligraphy from the Psalter of Ricemarch, 11th century.

VID
GLORIARIS
INMALITIA:
POTENSMI
SERILORDIA
DITOTADIE·
INSIDIAS COGITAVIT
LINGVA TVAS NOL
ACVA FALIEISDOLV

ornamental manner. The images lost none of their vigour through being transformed in this way. If anything, they gained a new potency.

In some of the early Gospel Books, the Evangelist was represented by a symbol rather than a portrait. These symbols were based on two prophetic passages in the Bible. One of them described a vision which had appeared to Ezekiel (Ezekiel I, 5-10) and the other referred to a scene from the Day of Judgement. In both cases, the text described 'four living creatures', which early Christians interpreted as a symbolic reference to the Evangelists. They took the form of 'four beasts full of eyes before and behind. And the first beast was like a lion, and the second beast like a calf, and the third beast had a face as a man, and the fourth beast was like a flying eagle. And the four beasts had each of them six wings about him; and they were full of eyes within; and they rest not day and night, saying Holy, holy, holy, Lord God Almighty' (Revelations IV, 6-8).

By convention, these four creatures also referred to Christ's incarnation (the winged man), His majesty (the lion, a regal beast), His role as the Saviour of mankind (the calf or ox, traditionally sacrificial animals) and the Ascension (the soaring eagle). The most widely accepted attribution of the symbols was laid down by St Jerome. He linked Matthew with the winged man, Mark with the lion, Luke with the ox or calf, and John with the eagle. Once again, however, the Celts did not fall into line immediately with this proposal. In the *Book of Durrow*, for instance, the lion was employed as the symbol of St John.

Celtic artists also portrayed the symbols in a number of different ways. Sometimes, they showed them in a comparatively realistic way while, at other times, they chose to emphasize their divine nature by adding wings and certain human characteristics. Thus, the paws or talons of the animals might be replaced by hands, while the creatures themselves were shown standing upright, in a human posture. In a few rare instances, the symbols might also be combined. The most celebrated example of this occurred in the *Trier Gospels*, where the four emblems were represented as a tetramorph. This was a composite figure, combining the head of a man with the hind quarters of the other three animals.

The remaining illustrations in the early Gospel Books offered much greater scope for the use of traditional La Tène decoration. The Carpet

Symbols of the four Evangelists, Book of Kells, c. 800.

Pages – leaves of parchment given over entirely to ornamental designs – were not invented by Celtic artists, but they became one of the outstanding features of Insular illumination. The concept was developed in the East, where the artists of several cultures were expressly prohibited from representing any living form, but it also suited the Celtic predilection for abstract patterns.

The same could be said for the decorative calligraphy, which became increasingly elaborate as the ambitions of Celtic illuminators increased. Once again, the practice of highlighting certain sections of text by using an enlarged or ornamental letter was already long-established. In the early Gospel Books, however, this trend evolved beyond all recognition. The scale and complexity of the decorations continued to grow until, in manuscripts such as the *Lindisfarne Gospels* and the *Book of Kells*, a complete page might be filled by a single word or a short phrase. In time, these virtuoso passages became associated with specific sections of text. The most spectacular examples of calligraphy were reserved for the Initial Pages – the folios with the opening words of each Gospel – and the Monogram Page.

The latter refers to the early passage in Matthew's Gospel, which follows a lengthy list description of Christ's descent from Abraham. This starts with an account of Christ's birth (Matt. I, 18), which many churchmen regarded as the true beginning of the New Testament story. For this reason, artists took pains to make it the most sumptuous page in the entire book. It is commonly termed the Monogram Page, because the text opens with Christ's name, which was normally abbreviated as 'XP' in most manuscripts.

The *Book of Durrow*

The oldest surviving Celtic manuscripts appear to date back to the late 6th century. Already, in the fragmentary remains of a Psalter known as the *Cathach of St Columba*, there are a few enlarged initials while, in the

Carpet page with double-barred cross, Book of Kells, c. 800.

equally slender vestiges of a Gospel Book at Durham, there are early examples of plaitwork. The latter bear comparison with the carving on the crosses of Carndonagh and Fahan Mura.

After these early signs of promise came the *Book of Durrow*, the first of the fully decorated Gospel Books. It probably dates back to around 680, despite a later inscription which recorded the legend that it was copied out by St Columba (c.521-597) in the space of 12 days. This, at least, confirms its place of origin as one of the Columban group of monasteries, though it is still unclear whether it was produced at Iona (its chief foundation), in one of the Irish houses, or in Northumbria. Certain textual peculiarities link it with the *Book of Kells*, which would favour the Iona argument, but this has to be balanced by stylistic considerations, where there are greater affinities with north-eastern Britain. In any event, the manuscript was in Ireland by the 10th century, when a special shrine was created for it. A century later, it had arrived at Durrow itself, one of the monasteries founded by St Columba.

The illuminations in the Durrow manuscript are interesting, because they point to a number of very different influences, which had not yet been assimilated into a single style. The chief focus of the decoration was on the Carpet Pages and the Evangelists' symbols. The former made extensive use of multicoloured interlacing, which far outshone any contemporary examples, even though the bands were broader and less subtle than in the Gospel Books of the next century. The finest of the Carpet Page designs, however, were those featuring on folios 3v and 192v. The first of these presented an elaborate arrangement of spirals within spirals, contained inside an attractive interlace border. The individual groups of spirals were linked to each other by a flowing motif, known as a trumpet spiral. This type of pattern is highly reminiscent of the ornamental metal discs, which were featured on the bronze hanging-bowls of the period.

The design of folio 192v is even more striking. Here, a central roundel, composed of plaitwork, is enclosed within a border of animal interlacing. Some of the creatures are clearly snakes, but the side panels show an unusual form of quadruped. Historians have drawn telling comparisons between these and a number of Anglo-Saxon artefacts, most notably the pommel of a sword from Crundale Down and a purse-cover from the Sutton Hoo ship burial.

The Evangelists' symbols conjure up an entirely different set of associations. The highly stylized man, who represents St Matthew (none of the Durrow symbols have either wings or halocs), can be likened to much of the stone-carving of the period. On the crosses of both Moone and Carndonagh, for example, it is possible to find figures whose torsos are conveyed by a simple, formless block. At the same time, the chequerboard decoration of the man's cloak may well have been inspired by the *millefiori* enamel inlays, which were something of a speciality of Irish metalworkers. The Durrow lion is equally interesting. The way that its legs and haunches appear to be attached by scrolled hinges is very close to the engraved depictions of animals on certain Pictish slabs, dating from the first half of the 7th century.

The *Echternach Gospels*

The achievements of the Insular illuminators did not remain confined to the British Isles. Missionaries from the Celtic Church travelled across to mainland Europe, taking with them some of the manuscripts that had been produced in their own scriptoria. These were copied, in turn, by monks on the Continent, thereby diffusing the influence of the Insular artists still further.

The *Echternach Gospels* provide a case in point. This intriguing manuscript was probably prepared for St Willibrord, shortly before his evangelical expedition to Frisia in 690. It contains a colophon, informing us that the text was copied from an exemplar which had been revised in 558 by Eugippius, the abbot of a monastery near Naples – confirmation that Celtic artists had access to books from the Continent. The impetus behind the Gospel Book may well have come from Willibrord's mentor, Egbert, who

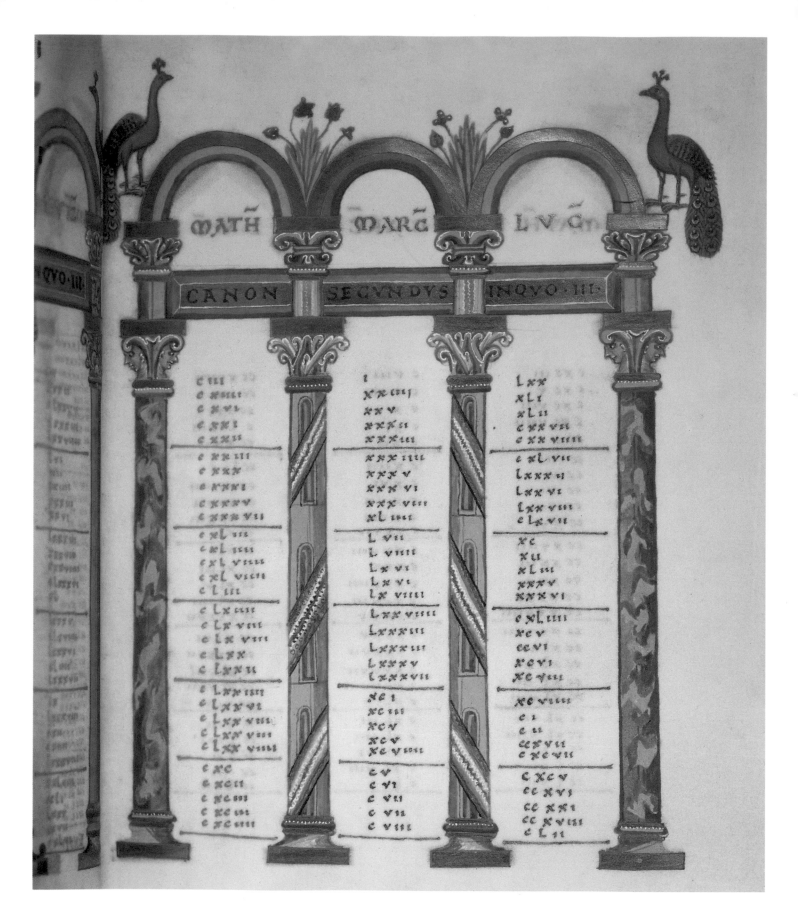

Canon Table, Echternach Gospel Book, c. 700.

was a keen advocate of Roman liturgical practices. More than 25 years had passed since these had been adopted officially at the Synod of Whitby, but many British and Irish priests still clung to the old ways. This could easily explain why the symbol of St Matthew wears the Roman tonsure, a rare sight indeed in Insular manuscripts. It was probably intended as a political statement.

Willibrord's mission was remarkably successful. He was appointed archbishop of the Frisians in 695, installing his see at Utrecht. Three years later, he founded the monastery of Echternach in Luxembourg. This was to prove an important artistic centre, producing many manuscripts in its own scriptorium.

As in the *Book of Durrow*, the Echternach Evangelists are represented by symbols rather than portraits. The symbol of Matthew offers the ultimate in stylization. His body is formed out of a series of loops, from which a pale head and tiny feet protrude. In his long, tapering hands, he displays a copy of his Gospel, the opening words of which are clearly legible. Behind him, is a rudimentary throne. The interlaced border, which owes something to the example of the *Book of Durrow*, extends towards the figure of the man, transforming him into the vertical shaft of a cross. St Mark's lion is the most attractive of the animal symbols. Its sinuous form is reminiscent of some Pictish carvings, but its elegant, prancing movement transcends any such sources.

The *Lindisfarne Gospels*

The *Lindisfarne Gospels* are almost contemporary with the Echternach manuscript. A 10th-century inscription by Aldred provides us with an unusually detailed description of the way that it was created and decorated over the years: 'Eadfrith, Bishop of the Lindisfarne church, originally wrote this book for God and for St Cuthbert and jointly for all the saints whose relics are in the island. And Ethelwald, Bishop of the Lindisfarne Islanders impressed it on the outside and covered it, as he well knew how to do. And Billfrith, the anchorite, forged the ornaments which are on the outside and adorned it with gold and with gems and with gilt-silver. And Aldred, unworthy and most miserable priest, glossed it in English between the

Head of St. Matthew (top left) and decorated initial (top right) from the Lindisfarne Gospels, c. 698.

lines.' This statement, which is generally assumed to be accurate, helps to date the manuscript to around 698, when Eadfrith became bishop. On balance, it seems likely that he would have worked on it before his appointment, when his duties would have been lighter.

The *Lindisfarne Gospels* mark a significant shift in the development of Celtic illumination. The influence of La Tène decoration is still very strong and, in the calligraphy and the ornamental pages, it reaches new peaks of sophistication. These elements, however, are now combined with images from a very different range of sources.

The change is most obvious in the portraits of the Evangelists. These stately figures are far removed from the stylized figures in the earlier Gospel Books, betraying a number of classical and Eastern influences. One specific source has long been identified. The figure of St Matthew bears a close resemblance to that of Ezra in the *Codex Amiatinus*, which was being copied out at Jarrow during the same period. Almost certainly, the two figures were taken from a common source. This is likely to have been one of the books, which were purchased from the library of Cassiodorus, a Roman author and scholar, and transported to Jarrow. The Lindisfarne artist, however, did not simply copy the picture. He borrowed the figure and combined it with a number of Byzantine motifs. This much is evident from the saints' names, which are written in Latinized Greek, and from the Greek style of their clothing.

The foreign inspiration of the Evangelists' portraits is further emphasized by the unusually complex imagery. In the portrait of St Matthew, for example, the identity of the figure on the right has been the source of much speculation. The halo confirms that he is holy and many commentators interpret him as the figure of Christ. According to this theory, the words that the Evangelist is writing help to draw aside a curtain in men's minds, thereby revealing the teachings of God.

The most Celtic elements in the *Lindisfarne Gospels* appear on the Initial Pages and the Carpet Pages. There are five of the latter, one at the start of the volume and one before each of the Gospels, and they constitute the finest achievement of the manuscript. Most are centred around the image of the cross, but they include a full repertoire of other motifs. On the opening Carpet Page, for instance, the cross and the adjacent panels are inlaid with a combination of fretwork and key patterns. Surrounding these, there are sections of interlacing, composed of much finer strands than in the *Book of Durrow* and arranged into a coloured grid. In the border, there is a running pattern, formed out of elongated birds which bite the claw or tail of their neighbour. The decoration is completed by interlaced projections at the corners, woven out of the ears of eight animal heads. Similar projections can be found on some of the jewellery of the period, most notably the Tara brooch.

The *Lichfield Gospels*

The innovations in the *Lindisfarne Gospels* met with a mixed reception. Some elements proved an inspiration to the next generation of illuminators, while others appear to have been quietly discarded. This much is evident from the *Lichfield Gospels*, a transitional work which stands midway between the Lindisfarne manuscript and the *Book of Kells*.

The origins of the *Lichfield Gospels* are unknown, although they are thought to date from the first half of the 8th century. By the next century, however, the book was in Wales. An inscription at the end of Matthew's Gospel informs us that 'Gelhi the son of Arihtuid brought this Gospel from Cingal and gave him his best horse for it.' This cryptic statement, which seems to imply that the manuscript was stolen or looted from the monastery that produced it, goes on to record that Gelhi donated his purchase to the church of Llandeilo Fawr in South Wales. The horse-trading may not have ended there for, by the 10th century, the book had been transported to Lichfield. There, it rapidly became linked with the name of St Chad, the local saint, and the manuscript is still occasionally described as the Gospels of St Chad.

The book has suffered considerable damage and has lost many of its illuminated pages. Even so, the remaining decoration suggests that the Lichfield artist was aware of recent developments in Northumbria. The layout of the only surviving Carpet Page bears a striking resemblance to that of the second Carpet Page in the *Lindisfarne Gospels*. A similar affinity is also shown in the placement of some of the Evangelists' symbols, which leap over the halo of the appropriate saint. On the other hand, there

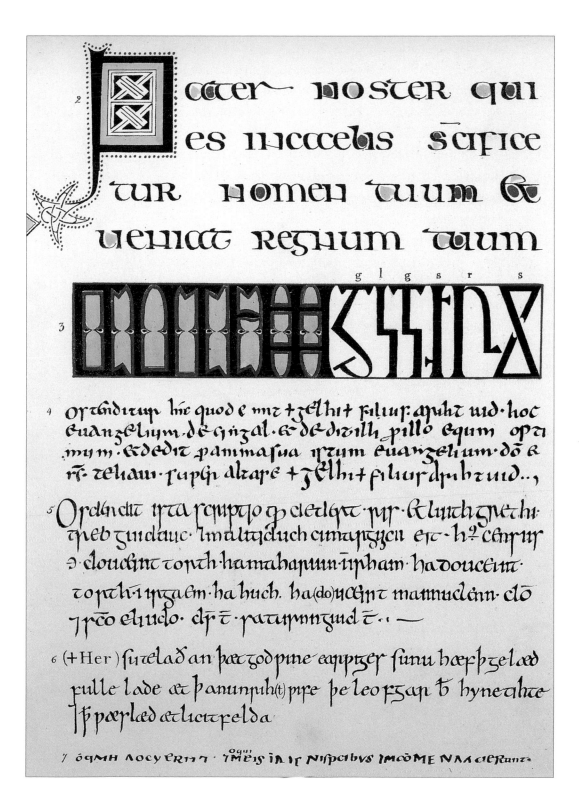

Lichfield Gospels, early 8th century.

has been no attempt to mimic the tepid naturalism of the Lindisfarne portraits. The languid Mediterranean figures have given way to the forceful stylizations preferred by Celtic artists. The portrait of St Luke, in particular, displays a rigid frontality and an intense, penetrating stare that is much closer in spirit to the powerful figures in the *Book of Kells*.

The illuminated pages at the start of St Luke's Gospel form the only ornamented section of the manuscript that has survived intact. From this, however, it is possible to gain a clear idea of the decorative scheme that was probably adopted. Luke's Gospel is prefaced with a portrait of the saint, a page with the four Evangelists' symbols, a Carpet Page, and an Initial Page, and it seems reasonable to assume that the other Gospels would have been treated in a similar manner. Such a programme would have been considerably more lavish than the ones employed in the early Gospel texts. Only in the *Book of Kells* was a more ambitious scheme attempted.

The *Book of Kells*

Despite its fame, the early history of the *Book of Kells* is obscure. Nothing certain is known about it before the early 11th century, when it was stolen from the church of Kells in the province of Meath. Fortunately, it seems that the thief's main interest lay in the book's rich binding, and the manuscript itself was retrieved some three months later. Like the *Book of Durrow*, it was traditionally associated with St Columba (d.597), even though it was clearly transcribed long after his death. In fact, it dates from around 800 and was probably produced at the island monastery of Iona. If so, its magnificence is all the more remarkable, for the manuscript was created at a time of great uncertainty. Iona suffered a series of Viking raids during this period and, in 814, most of the monks travelled across to Ireland, to take refuge in the newly established monastery at Kells. These disturbances may explain why the *Book of Kells* was never completed.

Even in its unfinished state, however, the *Book of Kells* is unquestionably the finest of the Insular Gospel Books. Each of the Gospels was prefaced

Canon Table, Book of Kells, c. 800.

with three pages of full-length decoration – a depiction of the Evangelists' symbol, a portrait of the Evangelist himself, and an Initial Page. In addition, there were extra pages of decoration at two key passages in the text, the incarnation of Christ and the Crucifixion. Last and most unusual of all, a series of narrative illustrations were planned, three of which have survived.

The emphasis placed on the Evangelists' symbols was unprecedented. In addition to the traditional symbol pages at the start of the Gospels, they featured in the Canon Tables, the portraits and other prefatory sections. They were also used in a number of different ways – sometimes as ornamental motifs, sometimes as heraldic beasts, and sometimes as potent talismans. As such, they underwent a variety of transformations. In one instance, a peacock's tail becomes attached to a lion's head while, in another, the eagle of St John holds the Gospel in a human hand. Only two of the portraits have survived, providing one of the weaker aspects of the decoration, but the four Initial Pages are superb. In each case, the first letter runs the full length of the page, and the words themselves are completely indecipherable to the untutored eye. Instead, the calligraphy becomes a pretext for a dazzling display of La Tène spiral and interlace designs. It also offers the artist an opportunity to exercise his imagination to the full. On the St John's page, for example, the letters 'c' and 'i' are transformed into a man playing a harp while, on the St. Luke's page, the characters 'iam' merge together to become an instrument of torture.

The decoration on the pages which mark the incarnation of Christ is even more spectacular. The format of the Monogram Page is similar to the examples in the Lindisfarne and Lichfield manuscripts, but the sheer profusion of detail is astonishing. Hidden away among the loops and spirals, there are vignettes of cats and mice fighting over a communion wafer, an otter clutching a fish, and a row of angels displaying the Gospels. In most other manuscripts, the Monogram Page provides the sole decoration at this point but, in the *Book of Kells*, the incarnation passage is commemorated with two other illustrations. There is a splendid Carpet Page – the only one

Virgin and Child, Book of Kells, c. 800.

in the Kells' manuscript – and a portrait of Christ. The latter was a great rarity in Insular manuscripts, as was the notion of adding decoration to the Crucifixion passage. Sadly, this is one of the sections of the book that was never completed. There is an ornamental Initial Page, but this faces a blank sheet where, doubtless, a depiction of the Crucifixion was planned.

The narrative illustrations hint at a new direction in Celtic art. With their preference for abstract or stylized forms, Celtic craftsmen usually shied away from themes of this kind and only a few, isolated examples can be found in the earlier Gospel Books. Here, there are three, and it seems likely that the complete manuscript would have included several more. The surviving illustrations depict the Temptation of Christ, the Arrest, and the Virgin and Child. The latter is particularly interesting, partly because it is the earliest-known version of this subject in an Insular manuscript, and partly because it demonstrates the hesitancy of an artist working in an unfamiliar genre. The figures of the Virgin, the Infant Christ and the attendant angels were probably borrowed from an Eastern icon, but they sit uneasily beside the more obviously Celtic elements – the writhing beasts in the border, the beard-tuggers in the semicircular insets, and the savage head on the back of the Virgin's throne.

Christian Metalwork

The paucity of surviving manuscripts underlines the terrible havoc that was wreaked by the Viking raiders. Both Lindisfarne and Iona were pillaged, and many precious books must have been destroyed in the process. These losses were purely incidental, of course, for the manuscripts themselves offered no real temptation for the invaders. They were much more interested in the ornate metal artefacts, which the monks used in their services and processions. Gold and silver objects had an immediate market value once they had been melted down, while the richly decorated bronze vessels could simply be used as ornaments. Shrines were emptied of their relics and turned into caskets. Similarly, eye-catching plaques and inlays were torn from croziers, lamps and ceremonial crosses, and became the

Ardagh chalice, Ireland, 8th century.

trophies of a successful raid. Viking graves of the period offer ample evidence of these practices.

Naturally, the monks did their utmost to protect the Church's property. Whenever there was time, the finest treasures were swiftly concealed. As a result, the best finds have come down to us through buried hoards. Two are especially notable. The Ardagh hoard was uncovered in 1868 by a young boy digging for potatoes. At a site near the Shannon estuary, he came across two chalices – one of them a superb example dating back to the 8th century – and four penannular brooches. This discovery was virtually unparalleled until 1980, when a selection of objects was found at Derrynaflan in County Tipperary. Among other things, this included a silver chalice, a silver paten with its stand, and a bronze strainer and basin.

The quality of these two hoards is variable, but the Ardagh chalice is universally recognized as one of the finest examples of Irish metalwork. It was formed out of two inverted bowls, and its sumptuous decoration demonstrates the wide range of techniques that were in use. There is intricate animal interlacing, conjured out of a mesh of gold filigree; there are studs of polychromed enamel (or, more accurately, cast glass); there are gilt bronze plaques with openwork designs; there are escutcheon plates on the handles, decorated with beaded wire and granules of gold; and there is a polished rock crystal, set into the base of the vessel.

One revealing facet of the Ardagh chalice is the band of engraving, which links the four plaques. This displays the names of the apostles, using a style of lettering that has been compared to the calligraphy in the Lindisfarne Gospels. More interestingly, perhaps, the names are given in a mixture of grammatical cases, suggesting that the craftsman may have been illiterate. By contrast, the silver paten from Derrynaflan – the finest of the items in the hoard – is marked with signs of an assembly code, which implies

PREVIOUS PAGES The Derrynaflan hoard, Ireland. The finds included an 8th-century paten and a 9th-century chalice.

The Lismore crozier, designed by Neachtain for Niall, Bishop of Lismore, Ireland, early 12th century.

literacy. This strengthens the theory that monastic workshops included both monks and secular artisans.

La Tène designs were not restricted to liturgical vessels. From an early stage, they were also used to adorn the croziers belonging to abbots and bishops. One of the oldest fragments is a crook, found at Ekerö in Sweden, which may date back to the 8th century. This features a number of animal heads, one of which has a human head clamped between its jaws – an image which can be found in the *Book of Kells* and other manuscripts of the period. Its socket is covered in a variety of enamel and *millefiori* patterns.

Initially, the principal decoration on croziers was confined to the crook and the knops. The latter are the bulbous metal collars, placed at intervals around the shaft. Most croziers had three or four of these. In general, they were made of cast bronze and featured engraved interlace patterns, sometimes highlighted with gold or silver foil. On later examples, elaborate animal ornaments were often added to the crook. These date from the very end of the Celtic period, when artefacts showed the increasing influence of Scandinavian styles. This is certainly true of the most famous Irish croziers, those from Clonmacnois and Lismore. On both of these, the animal interlacing and the crest on the crook are highly reminiscent of the Urnes style, which takes its names from the wood-carvings on a Norwegian church.

Shrines

On some croziers, most notably the one from Clonmacnois, the hook terminates in a bevelled panel, which conceals a tiny reliquary box. Beyond this, there is a theory that all the early Irish croziers were reliquaries – that they were originally designed as casings for the walking-sticks that had belonged to individual saints.

This is certainly possible, for the cult of the relic was very strong in Ireland, and many of the finest surviving items of metalwork are shrines of one sort or another. These were not intended solely for corporeal relics. As the diversity of designs suggests, they once housed a wide variety of

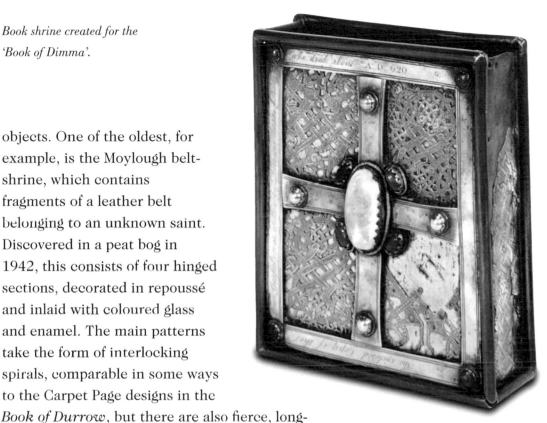

Book shrine created for the 'Book of Dimma'.

objects. One of the oldest, for example, is the Moylough belt-shrine, which contains fragments of a leather belt belonging to an unknown saint. Discovered in a peat bog in 1942, this consists of four hinged sections, decorated in repoussé and inlaid with coloured glass and enamel. The main patterns take the form of interlocking spirals, comparable in some ways to the Carpet Page designs in the *Book of Durrow*, but there are also fierce, long-snouted beasts, which bring to mind the animal engravings on the Ardagh chalice.

Not all shrines were directly linked to saints. The Irish Celts made a practice of preserving their most precious books and manuscripts in a portable shrine, known as a *cumdach*. This usually took the form of a box, inlaid with precious metals and gems. As such, it often fell prey to robbers and marauders. The cumdach enclosing the *Book of Kells* suffered this fate in 1006-7. A thief removed it from the sacristy of the church, stripped it of its gilded covering, and then discarded the manuscript itself. Without doubt, this was not an isolated case, for manuscripts such as the *Book of Durrow* and the *Book of Armagh* are known to have had their own shrines, which have long since vanished. Both of these were commissioned separately from the manuscript, and were presumably intended to enhance its prestige.

From surviving examples, it seems clear that the design of many book-shrines was closely related to the art of manuscript illumination. This can

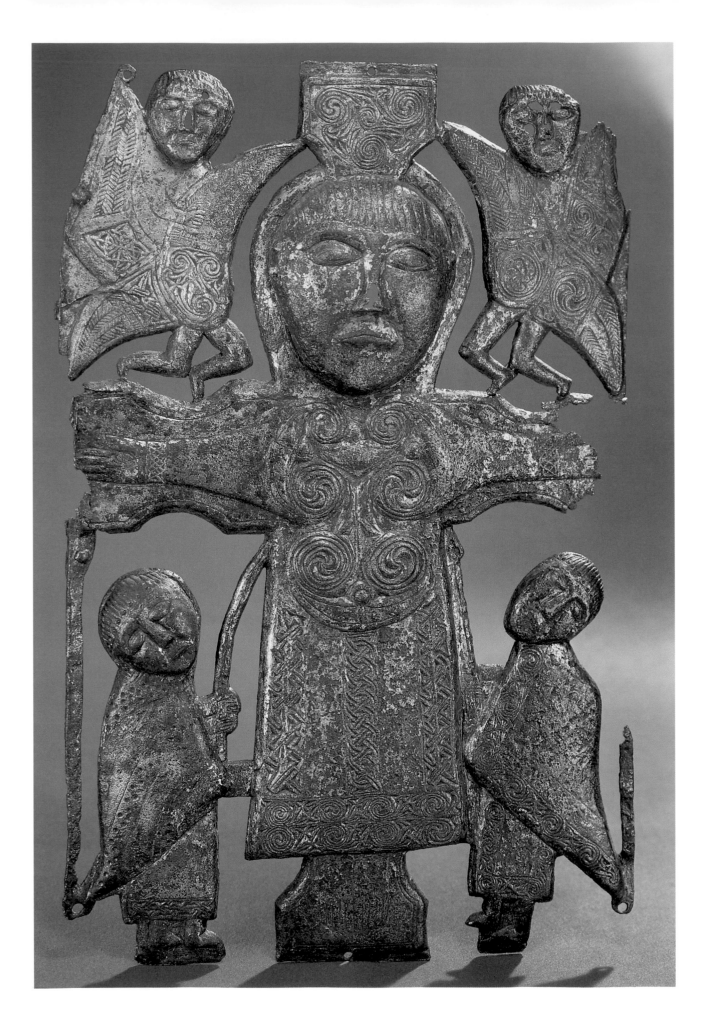

be seen from the *Soiscél Molaise* (the 'Gospel of St Molaise'), an 11th-century cumdach which was remodelled from the damaged remnants of an 8th-century casket. Its cover, fashioned out of silver and bronze, depicts the symbols of the four Evangelists arranged around the sign of the cross. This layout bears a close resemblance to illustrations in the *MacDurnan Gospels* and the *Book of Kells*. In particular, it is interesting to note how the creatures stand erect, their animal features combining with a human stance.

Most book-shrines and coverings appear to have been decorated with either the symbol of the Cross or else a Crucifixion. Chief among the latter is the marvellous scene on the Athlone plaque. This miniature masterpiece, made out of gilded bronze and measuring a mere 20cm, is thought to date back to the 7th century. Tiny holes in its outer edges indicate that it was once attached to the binding of a book.

The Crucifixion itself follows the format preferred by early Christians. This dictated that there was to be no emphasis on suffering; instead, Jesus was to be shown calm and majestic, attired in magnificent robes. Here, the eye is drawn immediately to Christ's huge head, which resembles the severed heads on Celtic phalerae and other pagan artefacts. The swollen cheeks and bulging eyes are typical La Tène stylizations. Angels hover on either side, their wings emblazoned with hatching and spiral patterns. Below, Stephaton and Longinus are depicted in ecclesiastical robes. The latter thrusts his lance into Christ's side, but Stephaton's sponge of vinegar is no longer visible and has presumably been lost. Christ's arms are articulated by spiral joints, and His regal attire is emphasized by a display of knotwork, spiral and key patterns. Above His head, a triple-spiral design symbolizes the Trinity.

For bodily remains, the most popular form of reliquary was the house-shaped shrine. Examples of these have been found not only in Britain and Ireland, but also in Italy, France and Scandinavia. The dearth of architectural evidence makes it hard to be certain of the precise source of inspiration for these, but it seems likely that they were based on early

The Athlone plaque, gilded bronze, Ireland, 7th century.

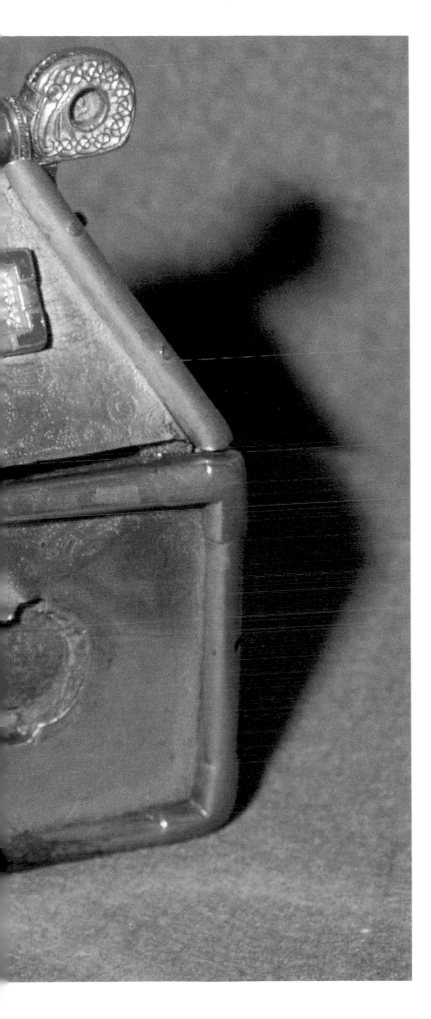

The Monymusk reliquary, a wooden casket with silver, bronze and enamel decoration, Scotland, c. 700. The shrine once held a relic of St. Columba and it was carried to the Battle of Bannockburn (1314) as a talisman.

chapels or tombs. The fact that, in the Kells' miniature of the Temptation of Christ, the temple of Jerusalem is represented by a very similar structure tends to strengthen the association with a church.

Most house-shaped shrines consisted of a wooden box covered in a sheet of precious metal, although a few were made entirely of metal. Decoration was focused on three areas: the ridge-poles attached to the top of the roof, the band around the eaves, and the sides of the casket. The first two were generally adorned with interlace patterns or beast-heads, while the latter was set with engraved roundels or gems. Typical examples include the Monymusk reliquary and the Emly shrine.

In addition, the Celts produced a number of shrines in the shape of bells. The most famous of these was reputedly designed to contain St Patrick's bell, the so-called Bell of the Will. It was specially commissioned in c.1100 by Donal O'Loughlin, an Irish king, and it is a fine example of the Celtic-Urnes style. The shrine consists of thick bronze plates, decorated with openwork patterns in gold filigree. These are punctuated with crystal and coloured glass insets.

A similar mix of styles can be seen on two other late shrines, the Cross of Cong and St Lachtin's Arm. The latter, which represents the saint's arm and clenched fist, is covered in a network of loosely woven interlace designs. These employ animal and plant motifs. The Cross of Cong is a much finer work. At first glance, it looks like a simple processional cross, but it was actually created to hold a fragment of the True Cross, which was set beneath the large crystal in the centre. The face of the shrine is divided into a series of panels, each decorated with a discreet maze of Urnes-style animals. A lengthy inscription confirms that the cross was made in c.1123 and names the artist as Maelisu, about whom nothing more is known. Most remarkable of all, however, is the stand on which the object rests. This takes the form of a beast's head, which clasps the sacred item between its fangs, offering the viewer a forcible reminder of the pagan roots of the Celtic style.

The Cross of Cong, Ireland, 12th century.

Stonework

The earliest Celtic stone-carvings in Ireland predate the Christian era. Five decorated monoliths have survived, the most famous of these being the Turoe stone in County Galway. This domed granite slab is covered in a flowing, curvilinear design, which is reminiscent of some contemporary metalwork. It is situated not far from a ringfort and burial site, but its precise purpose is uncertain. The carvings may have served some talismanic purpose or the stone itself may have been the focus of ritual activity.

In addition, the Celts made use of the striking megalithic formations that had been erected many centuries earlier. In particular, special reverence was accorded to the prehistoric sites of Newgrange and Tara. This can be deduced from the many references to them in early myths and stories. Newgrange, for example, was the home of the love god, Oenghus, and derived its name (literally, 'the cave of Grainne') from a leading character in the Fionn cycle of tales. Similarly, the site at Tara gained the reputation of being the ancient palace of the high kings of Ireland. According to tradition, the druids selected each new leader there, through a mystic ceremony known as the Tarbhfhess, and their choice was confirmed by one of the megaliths, the legendary Stone of Fál. This was said to have

Decorated kerbstone from Newgrange, Ireland, c. 3000 B.C.

Carvings on the Turoe Stone, Ireland, 1st century B.C./1st century A.D.

screamed aloud, whenever it was touched by the rightful successor to the throne.

Early missionaries did not seek to destroy the ancient stones, but they did try to harness their potent associations by Christianizing them. This was done by simply carving a cross on them, a practice that is said to have been inaugurated by St Patrick himself. Soon, Celtic evangelists were erecting their own monuments and adorning them with more ambitious designs. By the end of the 6th century, the first hints of the Celtic cross were beginning to appear. At Aglish in Co. Kerry, there is a pillar-stone which bears the symbol of a cross within a wheel, along with two swastikas and a series of Ogham markings (Ogham is an ancient Celtic alphabet). Also in County Kerry, there is the more roughly hewn pillar of Reask, where the wheel and cross are combined with a basic spiral design.

The next stage developed when artists made greater efforts to sculpt their stones into appropriate shapes. Two of the finest examples from this phase can be found at Fahan Mura and Carndonagh (both Co. Donegal). The first of these is a three-metre-high slab with a triangular peak. On it, the sign of the cross is formed out of broad-ribboned strands of interlacing. The design is not incised, as on earlier stones, but is sculpted in low relief. On one side, two armless figures are located beneath the cross-bar. Their meaning is unclear, but they may represent the Christian faithful or even church officials. On another Donegal stone, this time at Drumhallagh, two figures are shown in a similar position, wearing ecclesiastical dress and carrying croziers.

The main focus of interest on the Fahan slab, however, has been its inscription. In Greek uncial letters, this displays the Eastern form of the Gloria Patri, with its two extra words – 'glory *and honour* to the Father and to the Son and to the Holy Ghost'. Much speculation has arisen from this unusual form of words. Some see it as confirmation of links between Ireland and Spain, where the phrase was a standard feature of the mozarabic liturgy. More probably, it was copied from a Greek manuscript in a monastic library. Two possibilities are immediately apparent. The local monastery of Fahan Mura was a wealthy foundation, largely because St Mura was the patron saint of the powerful Northern Uí Néill family, and it would doubtless have had a sizeable collection of books. Alternatively, the

The Carndonagh Cross and accompanying slabs, Ireland, late 6th century.

cross may have been commissioned by the nearby community at Derry, which belonged to the Columban federation of monasteries.

On an artistic level, the cross at Carndonagh is even more important. Here, the stone itself was formed into the shape of a cross, and its surface was covered with a mixture of abstract and figurative decoration. Once again, the emblem of the cross is composed of thick interlacing but, on this occasion, the spaces beneath the transom are occupied by spiral patterns, formed by the beaks of three tiny birds – a typical piece of La Tène whimsy. On one side of the stone, the interlacing is confined to the upper part of the stone, while the shaft is decorated with three rows of men. The central figure is much larger than the rest and presumably represents Christ. His companions are too stylized to be identified with any certainty. Flanking the slab, there are two smaller stones, which also feature engraved figures. One is a warrior, armed with a shield and sword, while the other appears to be holding a harp. These have been interpreted tentatively as King David in his dual roles, as a soldier and as the author of the Psalms, but their exact meaning is far from clear.

The extent of the stylizations on early Irish slabs has created similar problems of identification elsewhere. A few of the more popular themes, however, can be discerned. Chief among these is the Crucifixion, which usually followed the format adopted on the Athlone plaque. Typical examples include the Duvillaun slab (Co. Mayo), where a naked Christ with fin-like arms is tormented by the tiny figures of Stephaton and Longinus, and the 8th-century slate slab from the Isle of Man, where Jesus is robed in a fine array of hatching and knotwork patterns.

On early monuments, Christ was also represented sometimes as a fish. This was one of the oldest Christian symbols, dating back to the era of persecution, when it was scratched on the walls of the catacombs in Rome. On Celtic stonework, it occasionally took the form of a fish with a man's head. Another device which occurs on a number of stones is a cross with a circular head, filled

The churchyard Cross at Aberlemno, Scotland, 8th century.

Cross-slab at St. Madocs, Scotland, 8th century.

with curved petal-like spokes, and a long, narrow stem. This may be a stylized version of the flabellum, a liturgical fan which was in common usage and which featured in several illustrations in the *Book of Kells*. The object bore a superficial resemblance to a cross and, because it was often made with peacock feathers – a conventional symbol of the Resurrection – it may have been deemed an appropriate subject for depiction.

Irish stonework designs were not confined to upright monoliths and crosses. They can also be found on recumbent slabs and tombs. For the historian, these are particularly helpful, since the inscriptions are often dated, or else include the names of figures whose dates are listed in the various Annals. One of the finest tombs, for example, commemorates St Berechtir, who died in 839. His grave in Tullylease, County Cork, is decorated with a patterned cross, formed out of five bell-shaped segments, which are highly reminiscent of one of the Carpet Pages in the Lindisfarne Gospels. The cross itself is filled with key patterns and the design also features five ornamented circles, perhaps representing the wounds of Christ.

Most of the decoration on Celtic tombs consists of a cross, formed out of interlacing or spirals, but a few other motifs can occasionally be seen. One of the most intriguing is a set of footprints, which indicates that the monk in question died while undertaking a pilgrimage. An example of this can be found at Iniscaltra, Co. Clare. The stones themselves were treated with great reverence and were deemed to have protective powers in their own right. Old slabs were frequently broken up and buried in fresh graves, so that the original 'owner' could intercede for the soul of the newly deceased. In 1955, excavations in the ancient cemetery at Clonmacnois revealed some 300 slabs that had been 'lost' in this way.

Celtic developments in stonework were mirrored elsewhere in the British Isles. In Northumbria, there was a similar taste for elegant high crosses, typified by the monuments at Ruthwell and Bewcastle. Their

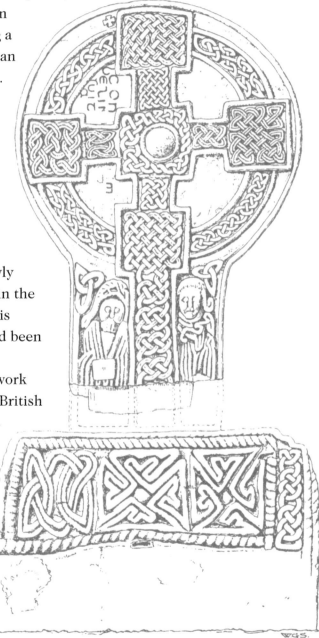

Damaged wheel-cross of Conbelin at Margham, Wales, 9th century.

decoration, however, was primarily inspired by Mediterranean models. The parallels with Pictish stonework are much closer. For, like the Celts, the Picts managed to create a remarkable fusion of pagan and Christian elements in their carvings.

The conversion of the Picts was initiated by St Columba, leading missionary expeditions from his base at Iona in the later years of the 6th century. Progress appears to have been slow, however, for the process was still incomplete in 710, when King Nechton contacted the abbot of Jarrow, asking for assistance on a variety of ecclesiastical matters. These links with Northumbria may help to explain the close affinities between Pictish stonework and some of the illustrations in Insular manuscripts. The similarities are particularly noticeable in the portrayal of animals, which were depicted with the same, distinctive spiral-joints.

The Picts' use of animal symbolism appears to owe much to their La Tène inheritance. Alongside this, however, they evolved an entirely different symbolic language. Many of their early slabs are marked with a combination of recognisable objects – combs, mirrors, tuning forks – and curious, abstract symbols, such as V-shaped rods and Z-shaped rods. No one is sure of the precise purpose of these enigmatic stones, though it may be that they served as territorial markers or personal memorials. According to the latter theory, the symbols identified the status and tribe of the deceased, along with the kinship of the person who had commissioned the monument.

Many of the symbol stones are thought to date from the 7th century, largely on the strength of their similarity to contemporary manuscripts. The majority of the Christian monoliths appear to have been produced in the following century. They featured the image of the wheel and cross but, unlike the Irish versions, they were not free-standing. Instead, the cross was carved in high relief on a slab. This enabled the craftsman to include a greater amount of decoration and also, perhaps, to ensure that the more

Hunting scene with a rare depiction of a woman riding side-saddle, Hilton of Cadboll stone, Scotland, 8th century.

secular elements were kept separate from the surface of the cross. On the slab at St Madoes, for example, the cross itself is adorned with knotwork and key patterns, while an array of fierce, biting animals is confined to the background.

A similar arrangement can be found on the famous cross-slab at Aberlemno. Spirals and plaitwork cover the cross, which is surrounded by a group of interlaced monsters. The most unique feature of the stone, however, can be found on the reverse of the slab. Here, two large symbols are placed above a detailed fighting scene. This is thought to represent the Battle of Nechtansmere (685), where the Picts defeated the Angles of Northumbria.

As mentioned, the classic format of the Celtic cross – the free-standing cross and wheel – developed in Ireland. The origins of this combination are unknown, although there is no shortage of potential theories. Some argue that the motif of the wheel, a widely used symbol for the sun, could have been borrowed from any one of a number of prehistoric cultures, while others maintain that it was meant to represent a halo (itself a form of sun symbol).

Another popular view is that it developed out of the exchange of ideas between metalworkers and stonemasons. Advocates of this theory suggest that inspiration may have come from the processional crosses of the period. In particular, they refer to monuments like the north cross at Ahenny, where the influence of metalwork is clear. At the precise points where the cross and wheel intersect, there is a series of prominent bosses, which strongly resemble metal rivets. Alternatively, the idea may simply have evolved from earlier depictions of the cross. Celtic designers loved to experiment with geometrical shapes and it is noticeable that, on some monuments, the cross was shown with semicircular terminals and a large circle at the point of intersection. It is quite possible that, at some stage, this central ring was expanded for purely aesthetic reasons.

The traditional high cross seems to have been firmly established by the 8th century. In its typical form, it offered craftsmen four main areas of decoration: the cross, the wheel, the pedestal, and the crown. This arrangement proved extremely versatile. On the north cross at Ahenny, for example, the principal surfaces are divided up into panels of abstract decoration, while the designs on the pedestal are figurative. These scenes are not easy to decipher, but they appear to include depictions of the mission of the Apostles, a holy procession and a hunting scene, which may allude to the spread of Christianity.

Elsewhere, the shape of the cross could be modified to accommodate a more ambitious programme. At Moone in County Kildare, for example, there is a very strange cross with a tall, narrow shaft and an enlarged pedestal. This is covered with a lengthy sequence of Biblical scenes, among them the Flight into Egypt, Daniel in the Lions' Den, and the Miracle of the

Moone Cross with the 12 Apostles at the base and, above them, the Crucifixion, Ireland, 9th century.

Loaves and Fishes. All of these are conveyed with an economy of form and an inventiveness that is highly appealing to modern eyes. Nowhere is this more apparent than in the depiction of the 12 apostles, who are shown with cube-shaped torsos and comic-strip heads.

For all their charm, however, the carvings on the Moone cross herald a significant shift in Celtic styles. The later Irish crosses display a growing taste for narrative Biblical scenes, portrayed in an increasingly naturalistic manner. This trend culminated in the marvellous high crosses of the 10th century, the outstanding examples being Muiredach's Cross at Monasterboice and the Cross of the Scriptures at Clonmacnois. These are superb achievements in their own right, but their links with the old La Tène tradition are tenuous in the extreme.

The popularity of Biblical stories on later monuments suggests that they were used as teaching-aids, as sermons in stone, when prayer meetings were held beside them. In addition, the outdoor crosses probably retained some of the protective aura that had been a feature of the pagan pillar-stones. A unique monastery plan in the *Book of Mulling* demonstrates how crosses were positioned strategically around the site, almost as a form of spiritual defence. Eight of them were placed outside, at the cardinal points of the compass; four dedicated to the Evangelists and four to the major Prophets. In addition, there was a Cross of the Holy Spirit by the sanctuary wall and three further crosses inside the enclosure.

The need for protection must have seemed all the more pressing as the Viking raids increased, sweeping away all the greatest treasures of the Church. Contemporary accounts described the ordeal in apocalyptic terms. They told of dreadful omens – fiery dragons and flashes of lightning in the sky – and of attacks so fierce that the relics of the saints were 'shaken out of their shrines'. In such a climate of fear, the last great monuments of the Celts may well have represented a supreme act of defiance and a symbol of their determination to survive.

Cross of the Scriptures, east side, Clonmacnois, Ireland, 10th century.

Glossary

Canon Table	Reference table in a Gospel Book, listing comparative sections of text
Carnyx	Animal-headed war trumpet
Carpet Page	Ornamental page in a Gospel Book, mainly consisting of abstract patterns
Champlevé	Enamelling technique, where vitreous powders are applied in narrow grooves and fused into place
Columban monastery	Monastery following the teachings of St Columba
Filigree	Decoration formed from soldered wires
Flabellum	Liturgical fan
Gospel Book	Manuscript containing the four Gospels
Hallstatt	Prehistoric period, named after an Austrian cemetery
Hatching	The use of finely engraved parallel lines to suggest shading
Initial Page	Page of ornamental calligraphy, often featured at the start of a Gospel
Insular	Produced in Britain or Ireland, as opposed to Continental Europe
La Tène	Prehistoric period, named after a Swiss archaeological site
Millefiori	Ornamental design formed by the fusion of coloured glass rods. Literally 'a thousand flowers'
Monogram Page	Page of ornamental calligraphy featuring Christ's monogram
Openwork	A pierced design, often in metalwork, where the pattern is formed by openings in the material
Palmette	Ornamental motif resembling a palm frond
Paten	A communion plate
Penannular Brooch	A ring-shaped brooch with a small gap in its hoop
Phalera	Ornamental bronze disc

Psalter	Manuscript containing the Book of Psalms
Repoussé	Relief design on metalwork, produced by hammering out the material from behind
Ritual Damage	The practice of damaging an object deliberately, as a form of sacrifice
Torc	Metal collar worn by high-ranking Celts
Triskele	Three-legged spiral motif
Tumulus	A burial mound
Urnes style	Style of decoration with characteristic animal-interlacing, named after the carvings at a Norwegian church

Bibliography

Arnold, Bruce   *Irish Art*, Thames & Hudson, 1969

Bryce, Derek   *Symbolism of the Celtic Cross*, Llanerch Publishers, 1989

The Celts – Exhibition Catalogue, Bompiani, 1991

Chadwick, Nora   *The Celts,* Pelican Books, 1970

De Hamel, Christopher   *A History of Illuminated Manuscripts,* Phaidon Press Ltd, 1994

Dillon M. & Chadwick N.   *The Celtic Realms,* Weidenfeld & Nicolson Ltd, 1967

Eluère, Christiane   *The Celts, First Masters of Europe,* Thames & Hudson, 1992

Finlay, Ian   *Celtic Art,* Faber & Faber Ltd, 1973

Green, Miranda   *Dictionary of Celtic Myth and Legend,* Thames & Hudson, 1992

Henderson, George   *From Durrow to Kells, the Insular Gospel Books 650-800,* Thames & Hudson, 1987

Henry, F.   *Irish Art in the Early Christian Period,* Methuen & Co. Ltd, 1940

Henry, F.   *Irish Art during the Viking Invasions,* Methuen & Co. Ltd., 1967

Laing, L. & J.   *Art of the Celts,* Thames & Hudson, 1992

Megaw, R. & V. *Celtic Art,* Thames & Hudson, 1989

Nordenfalk, Carl *Celtic & Anglo-Saxon Painting,* Chatto & Windus, 1977

Norton-Taylor, Duncan *The Celts,* Time-Life Books, 1974

Ritchie, Anna *Picts,* H.M.S.O., 1989

Romilly Allen, J. *Celtic Art,* Bracken Books, 1904

Ryan, Dr Michael *Metal Craftsmanship in Early Ireland,* Country House, 1993

Sandars, N.K. *Prehistoric Art in Europe,* Penguin Books Ltd., 1968

Sharkey, John *Celtic Mysteries,* Thames & Hudson, 1975

Picture credits

Photos by Peter Clayton: pp. 13, 21, 23, 31, 36, 37, 38, 42, 47, 48, 50, 55, 63, 73, 106-7, 119.

Photos by C. M. Dixon: pp. 111, 113, 121, 122.

Supplied by Bridgeman Art Library: back cover, p. 14 (British Museum), p. 17 (Rheinisches Landesmuseum, Bonn); p. 22 (Greek Museum, University of Newcastle upon Tyne), p. 32 (British Museum), p. 40)Museum of Antiquities, Newcastle upon Tyne), p. 56 (Lauros-Giraudon/Bridgeman Art Library), p. 58 (National Museum of Ireland), p. 67 (British Museum, London), p. 74 (Bibliotheque Nationale, Paris), p. 86 (British Library, London), p. 97 (National Museum of Ireland), p. 114 (private collection).

Supplied by Visual Arts Library: front cover, p. 6 (Musée Calvet), p. 8 (British Museum), p. 28 (British Museum), p. 35 (Musée des Antiquités Nationale, St Germain), p. 49 (Reims, Municipio), p. 52, pp 60-61 (Musée Archéologique, Châtillon-sur-Seine), p. 62, p.64, p.65 (Gloucester Museum), p.69, pp70-71(Musée des Antiquités Nationale, St Germain), pp 98-9 (National Museum of Ireland), p. 108 (National Museum of Ireland).

Supplied by the National Museum of Ireland, Dublin, pp 100, 104.

Index

Page numbers in italic refer to illustrations